RATIONALISM, EMPIRICISM, AND IDEALISM

British Academy Lectures
on the
History of Philosophy

SELECTED AND INTRODUCED BY

ANTHONY KENNY

CLARENDON PRESS · OXFORD
1986

Oxford University Press, Walton Street, Oxford OX2 6DP

Oxford New York Toronto
Delhi Bombay Calcutta Madras Karachi
Kuala Lumpur Singapore Hong Kong Tokyo
Nairobi Dar es Salaam Cape Town
Melbourne Auckland

and associated companies in
Beirut Berlin Ibadan Nicosia

Oxford is a trade mark of Oxford University Press

Published in the United States
by Oxford University Press, New York

British Library Cataloguing in Publication Data

Rationalism, empiricism and idealism: British
Academy lectures on the history of philosophy.
1. Philosophy, Modern
I. Kenny, Anthony   II. British Academy
190   B791
ISBN 0–19–824669–2
ISBN 0–19–824670–6 Pbk

Library of Congress Cataloging in Publication Data
Main entry under title:
Rationalism, empiricism, and idealism.
Chiefly lectures delivered at the British Academy.
Includes index.
1. Philosophy, Modern—Addresses, essays, lectures.
I. Kenny, Anthony John Patrick.   II. British Academy.
B791.R33 1986   190   85–15469
ISBN 0–19–824669–2
ISBN 0–19–824670–6 (pbk.)

Printed in Great Britain
at the University Printing House, Oxford
by David Stanford
Printer to the University

CONTENTS

NOTE ON CONTRIBUTORS

ANTHONY KENNY is Master of Balliol College, Oxford

MICHAEL AYERS is Fellow and Tutor in Philosophy at Wadham College, Oxford

JOHN PASSMORE is Professor of Philosophy at the Australian National University, Canberra

IAN HACKING is Professor of Philosophy at the University of Toronto

HIDÉ ISHIGURO is Professor of Philosophy at Barnard College, New York

G. E. M. ANSCOMBE is Professor of Philosophy in the University of Cambridge

DAVID PEARS is a Student of Christ Church, Oxford

LORD QUINTON is President of Trinity College, Oxford

RICHARD WOLLHEIM is Professor of Philosophy at Columbia University, New York

INTRODUCTION

by Anthony Kenny

George Dawes Hicks, Professor of Philosophy at the University of London, left provision in his will for an annual lecture, to be given under the auspices of the British Academy, on 'subjects relating to the History of Philosophy, either ancient or modern'. The first lecture in the series, 'Bergson on Morality' was given by F. C. Copleston in 1955.

All but one of the lectures in this volume were delivered some time in the last fifteen years of the British Academy as Dawes Hicks lectures. The one exception, Professor G. E. M. Anscombe's lecture on 'Times, Beginnings, and Causes' was delivered as a Henriette Hertz philosophical lecture to the Academy. All the lectures are concerned with the history of modern philosophy between the seventeenth and twentieth centuries.

For textbook and examination purposes, seventeenth- and eighteenth-century philosophers are commonly divided into rationalists and empiricists. The rationalists, we are told, believed that reason, rather than experience, gave us knowledge of the essences of things; they thought that knowledge could be laid out in a single deductive system. Empiricists, on the other hand, thought that all knowledge was based on experience and there were no innate ideas; far from being a systematic and unified whole, the world accessible to our knowledge was atomic and disconnected. To make the compartments conveniently watertight, the rationalists Descartes, Spinoza and Leibniz were continentals, while the empiricists Locke, Berkeley and Hume were obliging enough to live in the British Isles and write in English.

Several of the contributors to the present collection make clear how misleading is the curricular distinction between rationalists and empiricists. A close reading of any philosopher on either side of the line reveals nuances which show an awareness of the truths stressed by those on the other side. From the viewpoint of either the thirteenth or the twentieth centuries, the presuppositions which are shared by Descartes and Locke are more important than the issues which divide them.

It is not just that the founding fathers of rationalism and empiricism set out from a common starting point in the intellectual geography of the seventeenth century. Hidé Ishiguro, who subtitles her lecture 'A reconsideration of the distinction between rationalism and empiricism', shows how at the other end of the story too, Leibniz and Hume, who are often taken to stand at the extreme points of rationalism and empiricism respectively, can be represented as standing remarkably close together even on the great dividing issue of causation.

The first six essays in this volume are all concerned with philosophers commonly brought within the rationalist or empiricist camp; they all illustrate to a greater or less degree how much those in each camp shared problems, and often answers, with each other.

Michael Ayers discusses Locke's thesis that all our ideas are either simple ideas or else complex ideas constructed out of simple ideas. This compositional model, he argues, does not derive from contemporary corpuscular physics; it has its roots in Aristotelian logic, and has much more in common with Descartes's methodological pursuit of simple ideas which could be clearly and distinctly perceived.

Though Descartes and Locke sometimes hold similar language about the apprehension of simple and complex ideas, their doctrine of belief is often contrasted. Descartes believed that assent to a proposition was voluntary, an act of the will. Locke said roundly 'to believe this or that to be true is not within the scope of our will'. J. A. Passmore, in his lecture 'Locke and the Ethics of Belief' shows that we have here not so much a contrast between Descartes and Locke as a tension within Locke himself. For Locke thought we were obliged to proportion our belief to the evidence, and he wanted to blame, and therefore hold responsible, those who gave credence to preposterous religious beliefs. Passmore documents Locke's attempts to reconcile these two theses, and shows how his account of belief gradually changed as he gave up the ideal of human beings as automatically rational in the face of the experience of the irrational enthusiasms of the Puritan sectaries.

'Leibniz knew what a proof was. Descartes did not.' Thus Ian Hacking begins his lecture on proofs and eternal truths. Leibniz thought that truth is constituted by proofs. Descartes thought proof irrelevant to truth: the God who creates the eternal truths is no prover. Both Descartes and Leibniz, Hacking claims, are responding to an intellectual malaise caused by the way in which the recent scientific revolution had turned upside-down the Aristotelian ideal of science as a grasp of universal first principles concerning essence and cause and the true being of things. We are wrong, he suggests, to see rationalist philosophers as concerned fundamentally with epistemology. For them the basic question is not 'How can we know?' but 'What is truth?'

Hidé Ishiguro, as I have said, is anxious to illustrate the unhelpful nature of the grouping of philosophers into rationalists and empiricists. All the philosophers so grouped believed that experience was necessary but not sufficient for knowledge of the external world. If empiricism is supposed to be the doctrine that all knowledge of the world comes from sense perception alone, and if rationalism is supposed to mean that knowledge of reality comes from our understanding independently of the data of our senses, both are positions held by no one and better forgotten. On the key issue of causation, Ishiguro shows, Leibniz's theory of pre-established harmony has surprising resemblances to Hume's theory of constant conjunction. There is, however, a real distinction to be drawn between thinkers who regard it as essential to place scientific regularities within a general picture of the structure of the universe, and those who collect regularities without linking what is observed to any general concept of reality. This does indeed represent a difference of spirit between a rationalist such as Leibniz and an empiricist such as Hume.

Professor Anscombe, like Miss Ishiguro, devotes much of her lecture to a consideration of Hume's opinions on causation. She is mainly interested, however, not in Hume's contention that causal relations are concomitances without any logical link between cause and effect, but rather in his doctrine that 'Every beginning of existence has a cause' has no logical necessity about it. She dissects the proof which Hume offers of this claim, and deploys against Hume an argument derived from Hobbes to the effect that a thing's coming into existence at a time and in a place cannot be made intelligible without reference to a causal origin. If we try to suppose that some object has come into existence without a cause, we have no reason to assign one time and place to this coming into existence rather than another. Hume's contention therefore fails.

David Pears's lecture considers the question whether Hume's acount of the understanding offers a successful empiricist alternative to rationalism and scepticism. Like Anscombe and Ishiguro, he considers Hume's analysis of causation, but he is interested in the explanation of the origin of causal belief as one which was designed to fit into a more general theory of the origin of certain problematical beliefs. The general theory is that belief is an idea endowed with vivacity through its association with a present impression, and that such associations are produced by the three natural relations, resemblance, continguity, and causation. Pears illustrates, in a sympathetic manner, the ambiguities and confusions in this theory, and Hume's own dissatisfactions with it. He concludes that Hume was right to think that the theory in the end fails, but it is, he claims, a noble failure: 'there is more philosophy in it than in many more successful enterprises.'

Kant's critical idealism endeavoured to incorporate and supersede the insights of both rationalists and empiricists. Knowledge of his work quickly spread to Britain, but there was no school of British Kantians. In the 1860s the dominant philosophical groups were the school of experience, of which John Stuart Mill was the senior luminary, and the school of intuition, deriving from the Scottish philosophy of common sense and presided over by H. L. Mansel in succession to Sir William Hamilton. Anthony Quinton in his lecture chronicles panoramically how Hegelian Idealism, first orally communicated to his pupils by Benjamin Jowett, then promulgated here in writing in Stirling's book *The Secret of Hegel*, rapidly became dominant in British Universities, and retained key posts in the academic establishment until the Second World War.

Richard Wollheim, in the final lecture in the volume, takes his point of departure from the second generation of British Hegelianism: his subtitle is 'The Moral psychology of British Idealism and the English school of Psychoanalysis compared.' His essay is largely a comparison between the theories of moral development put forward by F. H. Bradley and Melanie Klein. He apologizes to the memory of Dawes Hicks for taking philosophy to include moral psychology. The apology is made partly with tongue in cheek, because Wollheim makes clear that he thinks the boundary between philosophy and psychology is a dubious one. Many of his colleagues might feel that if any apology is due, it is not for crossing the frontier between philosophy and psychology, but for trespassing into areas of psychology whose methodology and scientific status is highly suspect to many philosophers. But Wollheim's trespass is deliberate, fully aware of the hostile scrutiny of many in the analytic tradition within which he can himself move so skilfully. His lecture is evidence of a conviction, which is surely justified, that philosophy can never fully illuminate or excite unless it is prepared to leap over the boundaries which in its critical moods it sets up for itself.

All these lectures illustrate a characteristic of contemporary

British historical work in philosophy. Compare any British essay in the history of philosophy with its Continental or American counterparts, and you will find many fewer footnotes, less complete bibliographies, less engagement with the secondary literature. This sometimes gives the impression—and indeed sometimes justifies the impression—that British history of philosophy lacks scholarly substance and is in constant danger of anachronism. Against that criticism there is a great merit to be set, which is illustrated in this volume. When these writers address a problem in the history of philosophy it is not in any antiquarian spirit: it is because they believe that the attempt to reach up to the great minds of the past is one of the best ways of gaining illumination about the nature and problems of philosophy itself.

LOCKE'S LOGICAL ATOMISM

By MICHAEL AYERS

ALL our ideas are either simple ideas or else complex ideas constructed out of those simple ideas. What made Locke adopt this compositional model for thought? The answer seems to go without saying. Compositionalism seems no more than the natural model for anyone who wants to claim that all our ideas come from experience. It seems only natural to explain the idea of a centaur, which cannot have been acquired in experience, as a fiction constructed out of elements which have been so acquired. It seems only natural that Locke should have tried to extend that explanation to the ideas of God and infinity, to mathematical ideas, to the ideas of material and spiritual substance, to the ideas of right and wrong, and to other ideas commonly held to be innate in his time because they seemed to transcend experience or to be independent of it. Yet to stop there is to fail to discern the full meaning of compositionalism for Locke, the special significance of 'simple' and 'complex' in his philosophy.

One proposal as to such a deeper meaning may appeal to some just because it finds the source of Locke's model outside the abstractions of pure philosophy. That is the view, given graphic expression by Sir Isaiah Berlin, that Locke was captivated by the methods of contemporary physics. Just for that reason, Berlin suggests,

> The mind was treated as if it were a box containing mental equivalents of the Newtonian particles . . . These 'ideas' are distinct and separate entities . . ., literally atomic, having their origin somewhere in the external world, dropping into the mind like so many grains of sand inside an hour glass; there they continue in isolation, or are compounded into complexes, in the way in which material objects in the outer world are compounded out of complexes of molecules and atoms.[1]

A similar suggestion has recently been made by Dr M. A. Stewart, of Lancaster University. Stewart argues, I am sure rightly, against

[1] I. Berlin (ed.), *The Age of Enlightenment* (1956), p. 31.

those eminent commentators[1] who have claimed that compositionalism became, in later editions of the *Essay*, a somewhat half-
hearted component of Locke's concept-empiricism. He offers
evidence that even in his latest thoughts Locke enjoyed finding
rather detailed analogies between his theory of ideas and Robert
Boyle's theory of particles or corpuscles. For Stewart, so it seems,
the question whether Locke remained faithful to compositionalism just is the question whether he continued to take the analogy
with physics seriously.[2]

There is one big problem with this story. No doubt every
thinker, however revolutionary, has to work within a tradition
using, for whatever fresh purposes, the conceptual tools supplied
by his context. But conceptual tools are not just words and
phrases. For a philosopher, to construct a theory by means of such
tools and to define his relationship to the tradition is one and the
same act. Even to refuse to employ certain available concepts is a
positive contribution to the latter task. If it is true that Locke took
over the notion of combination from physical theory, then one
must expect some intelligible relation between that theory and
what he saw himself as doing. One might, for example, expect—to
be rather obvious—that he took himself to be offering a theory of
the mind with the same status as Boyle's theory of matter. The
trouble is that we know just how he saw himself in relation to
Boyle, because he tells us, and it has nothing to do with any
analogy between simple and complex in 'the material and intellectual worlds'.[3]

Boyle's method included two distinct components, experimental and theoretical. The first, generally known as 'natural
history', was a process of observation and experiment leading to
empirical or merely descriptive generalization such as, indeed,
Boyle's Law. The second consisted in speculative and usually
rather general explanation in accordance with the hypothesis of
corpuscles and the void. This speculation was valuable in
explaining how material variety and change might arise from a
few simple principles. Yet it is to 'natural history' that Boyle's
specific discoveries were credited. Now consciousness for Locke is
an attribute of the mind or thinking thing at the level of observa-

---

[1] Cf. J. Gibson, *Locke's Theory of Knowledge* (1917), ch. iii; R. I. Aaron, *John
Locke* (2nd edn., 1955), ch. iii.

[2] M. A. Stewart, 'Locke's Mental Atomism and the Classification of Ideas',
I and II, *Locke Newsletter*, 1979 and 1980. See especially II, pp. 46–60.

[3] The phrase is adapted from *Essay Concerning Human Understanding*, ed.
P. Nidditch (1975), II. xii. 1.

tion: the real and underlying nature or essence of 'that which
thinks' is unknown, a matter for speculation.[1] He sees his theory of
ideas and knowledge as the application of what he calls the
'historical, plain method' to the experienced operations of the
mind.[2] Consequently, whereas absolutely simple material particles would be ontologically or, to use Berlin's word, 'literally'
atomic, simple ideas are only 'simple' at the superficial level of
appearance and mere description. That is why Locke disclaims
any Cartesian intention to 'meddle with the Physical Consideration of the Mind' ('physical' here meaning 'natural' rather than
'material'.)[3] He even refuses to arbitrate between materialism and
immaterialism as explanations of the natural basis of consciousness.[4] The theory of material atomism itself was for Locke far from
perfect, although a hypothesis for which he fears 'the Weakness of
humane Understanding is scarce able to substitute another'.[5] All
this is part and parcel of the strong anti-dogmatism which constitutes a major theme of the *Essay*. It is therefore incredible that
he was predisposed by any respect for Boyle's method to find the
structure of Boyle's speculation replicated at the level at which we
observe or experience the mind.

In other words, the analogy between the composition of ideas
and the composition of physical particles does no theoretical work
for Locke, but arises as little more than a decorative conceit. Its
elaboration may be significant if we are interested in the literary
style or tone of the *Essay*, a not unimportant topic, but we should
look elsewhere for the answer to the question with which we
began. I would suggest that we should look, not towards physics,
but less adventurously at the context of existing logic and
epistemology. For the truth is that these branches of philosophy
had been heavily compositionalist since Plato.[6] It is that background which gives the compositionalism of the *Essay* its philosophical depth and significance, making it the vehicle by means of
which Locke could express systematic opposition, above all, to the
followers of Aristotle and Descartes. He does so, very crudely

---

[1] Cf. *Essay*, II. i. 9; IV. iii. 17; IV. iii. 29; IV. vi. 14; IV. xii. 12; etc.

[2] *Essay*, I. i. 2.

[3] Ibid.

[4] Cf. *Essay*, IV. iii. 6.

[5] *Essay*, IV. iii. 16.

[6] Cf. *Theaetetus* 203, where Plato uses the alphabet analogy employed by
Locke at *Essay*, II. vii. 10. Although Stewart may well be right that Locke got
the idea from Boyle (who follows Lucretius in using it to expound physical
atomism) it seems possible that seventeenth-century compositionalism is
directly indebted to the argument of *Theaetetus*.

speaking, by arguing that what is a paradigm of simplicity for the rival theory is in fact complex; or that what is held by others to be self-evidently complex, is better regarded as simple.

It seems that the doctrine which was uppermost in Locke's mind when he first began to set out the theory of the *Essay* (in what is now known as 'Draft A')[1] was the Aristotelians' notion of a simple term or 'simple apprehension'. That notion arises in the context of Aristotelian theories of the proposition, in which predication was regarded in three associated ways as it pertains to words, to things, and to thoughts. First, in predication words or terms are combined in sentences. Such combination, Aristotle tells us, must at least implicitly include a verb, paradigmatically the verb *to be*, before something capable of truth or falsity is achieved.[2] Second, we are also invited to regard the proposition as the association of things or beings or entities. For example, the species *man* may be said or predicated or affirmed of the individual man; and one thing, its quality *white*, exists 'in' another thing, the white object.[3] Third, Aristotle takes it that something corresponds in the mind to both these levels, a thought which does not differ from nation to nation as language differs.[4] For later Aristotelian theory the act of mind which corresponds to a term is the 'simple apprehension' of its meaning, or a 'concept'. 'Judgement' or mental 'affirmation' corresponds in the mind to the ordering or combination of terms in the sentence or statement. Sentences or propositions can in turn be combined in syllogism, and judgements or affirmations, correspondingly, in reasoning, 'ratiocination', or 'mental discourse'. Hence logic was traditionally divided into three parts, concerned with terms, with propositions, and with syllogism.

This straightforward model of increasing complexity seems to have had, right from its origin in Aristotle himself, an interesting qualification relating to the first stage. The chief part of Aristotle's theory of terms is his doctrine of 'categories' or 'predicaments' which distinguishes various sorts of predicate or, if you like, of being or attribute. 'Man', 'horse', 'gold' fall under the category of substance; 'four-foot' falls under quantity; 'white', 'musical' under quality; 'larger' under relation; 'in the Lyceum' under place; and so forth. Each of these predicates was held to be simple,

---

[1] *Locke's Essay: An Early Draft* (1936), eds. R. I. Aaron and J. Gibb (written 1671). (Henceforth 'Draft A'.)

[2] Cf. *De Interpretatione*, 17a11-15.

[3] Cf. *Categoriae*, ii.

[4] Cf. *De Int.* 16a3-9.

however many words it may contain. It is incapable of truth or falsity by itself, without combination.[1] Yet this conception of simplicity, tying it to the categories, leaves open the possibility of compounds which combine items from different categories but which are not straightforwardly or fully propositional. For example, 'musician' combines *man* and *musical*. Like any term, such expressions assert nothing by themselves, yet their compound nature shows itself in predication. 'John is a musician' means the same as 'John is a man and John is musical'.[2]

Here we may ask why the term 'man' is the paradigm of simplicity if, as Aristotelians believed, it can be defined, for example as *rational animal*. Their answer is that 'man' denotes a *thing* which is simple and unitary, while 'musician' does not. 'A man', 'a horse', 'gold', 'lead' answers the question 'What is it?' asked of a natural individual or naturally homogeneous quantity of stuff. That is to say, it classifies the individual or stuff according to its whole unitary nature or essence, rather than just by its size or quantity, or by its qualities or relations and so forth. It places the individual in a natural kind or species. (This narrow but natural understanding of 'What is it?' is perhaps more natural in Greek.) The unitary nature or essence of the species is expressed in a 'real', that is to say, scientific definition: *man* was commonly defined as *rational animal*. But that nature is supposed not to have parts corresponding to the linguistic parts of the definition. Musicians, by contrast, do not as such belong to a species with an essence, but rather to a class arrived at by arbitrary combination. Correspondingly musicians are not natural individuals *qua* musicians but *qua* human beings. To come or cease to be a musician is not to come or cease to exist.

This distinction is elaborated in the theory of predicables, the explanation-schema of Aristotelian science and another way of dividing up and relating predicates. The predicables are (after Porphyry) genus, species, difference, property, and accident. The 'real' or 'simple' definition of the essence of the *species* is by *genus* and *difference*. *Properties* are attributes common to all members of the species: they flow from, or are explained by, the essence, as our having hands or language or the capacity for laughter was supposed to flow from our being rational animals. *Accidents* are attributes which are not so connected with the essence, and which any member of the species may have or lack, as it chances. Thus there could be no single word which meant *man who is rational* or

---

[1] *Cat.* iv.
[2] Cf. *Metaphysica*, *Z* iv; *De Int.* v, viii, and xi.

man who has hands, since these conceptions or expressions add nothing to *man*. To try to introduce such a word would simply introduce a synonym for 'man', another name for the species. 'Musician', by contrast, does add to *man*, just because musicality is an accident.[1] The paradigmatic Aristotelian compounds thus compound substance with accident.

In the Port Royal *Logic*, a work in which Antoine Arnauld attempts to graft the Aristotelian logical tradition on to Cartesian metaphysics and epistemology, the Aristotelian distinction between simples and compounds seems to be given recognition in a discussion of complex expressions, in which 'two or more words are joined together to express one idea'. All such expressions are treated as quasi-propositional: the notion of a 'transparent body' is the notion of a 'body which is transparent'. But a distinction is drawn between explicative complex expressions, like 'man who is an animal endowed with reason', and determinative complex expressions, like 'transparent bodies'. In the former, the relative clause adds nothing and leaves the extension of the term unaffected. In the latter, the adjective or clause is an addition which further restricts the extension—there are fewer transparent bodies than bodies. But the whole explanation notably avoids recourse to Aristotelian ontology or epistemology. There is no appeal to a conception of man as a simple being, or of 'rational animal' as a simple definition. 'Man who is rational' is an explicative complex expression just because 'man' means the same as 'animal which is rational', which is a determinative complex expression.[2]

Locke's attitude to the Aristotelian theory is similarly reductive, but more elaborate and more explicit. His theory of ideas is essentially a theory of terms. Ideas are, in effect, Aristotelian 'simple apprehensions': that is to say, they constitute that which corresponds in the mind to terms or 'names', to expressions capable of standing in subject or predicate place. Ideas, he tells us in Draft A, are joined or separated 'by way of affirmation or negation, which when it comes to be expressed in words is called proposition, and in this lies all truth and falsehood'.[3] In the *Essay* he asserts that '*Is*, and *Is not*, are the general marks of the Mind, affirming or denying', and he draws attention to those other 'Words, whereby [the Mind] signifies what connection it gives to the several Affirmations and Negations, that it unites in one

---

[1] Cf. *De Int.* 20b31–21a8.

[2] *Logic, or the Art of Thinking* (1662), I. vii. (*Later note*: This paragraph now seems misleading. A more direct response to Aristotelian compounds is the category of *choses modifiées* of *Logic* I. ii.)   [3] 'Draft A', pp. 19–20.

continued Reasoning or Narration', for example 'but', 'therefore', and so on.[1] Here he is following closely in the tradition, treating the language of the second and third parts of logic in due place. He is famous for his supposed principle that all words stand for ideas,[2] but it is in fact essential to his theory that he is in agreement with earlier logicians that some words, 'which are not truly, by themselves, the names of any Ideas, are of . . . constant and indispensible use in Language'.[3]

Locke's classification of ideas as 'ideas of substances', 'simple ideas', 'ideas of simple modes', 'ideas of mixed modes', and 'ideas of relations' should therefore be read as, above all, a rival to the Aristotelian categories. Since there were ten or eleven of the latter he has at least achieved a striking economy. But it is equally striking that only one of his categories is allowed to be truly simple, namely simple ideas, ideas of simple modes being simple only by courtesy and in a limited sense. The relationship to Aristotelian theory, however, is quite explicit. For example, bearing in mind the logic-books' definition of a 'simple apprehension' as the understanding of a term, he tells us in Draft A that those simple ideas 'are properly simple apprehensions to which we apply the names that others doe'[4]—a point considerably less crude than a straightforward identification would have been. The first active composition of simple ideas, we are told, is the formation of specific ideas of substances. It is entirely unsurprising that Locke sees this composition as propositional: as he puts it, 'the first affirmation or negation of our minds are about those material objects in the frameing of our Ideas of them'.[5] He thought that in forming the complex idea of a species of thing out of simple ideas of sensible qualities we 'in effect'[6] affirm that the qualities do in general exist together in the same substance: 'yet the whole compounded idea being knowne under one name and taken altogeather considerd as one thing as man horse water lead etc they may be treated of as simple apprehensions'—that is, as single concepts corresponding to terms.[7] He is thus attacking the Aristotelian view of the names of the species of substances as paradigmatically simple terms from within an Aristotelian conception of complexity. To unpack

---

[1] *Essay*, III. vi. 1–2.

[2] Cf. *Essay* III. ii. 2: '*Words in their primary or immediate Signification, stand for nothing, but the Ideas in the Mind of him that uses them.*' At the end of the previous chapter he more accurately promises to consider, 'To what it is that Names . . . are immediately applied'.

[3] *Essay*, III. vii. 2.

[4] 'Draft A', p. 14.

[5] Ibid., p. 5.

[6] Ibid., p. 7

[7] Ibid., p. 17.

what is understood by the name is to unpack a quasi-propositional compound.

In the *Essay* Locke drops the suggestion that the complexity of complex ideas is propositional, for reasons which we need not go into. What does quite emphatically remain is the contrast with Aristotelian theory. Simply to entitle his chapter 'Of our Complex *Ideas* of Substances' was to throw down the gauntlet to the Aristotelians, but the contrast is immediately spelt out. The famous, much misunderstood passage which opens the chapter constitutes an insulting diagnosis of their error:

> The Mind . . . takes notice . . . that a certain number of . . . simple *Ideas* go constantly together; which being presumed to belong to one thing, and Words being suited to common apprehensions, and made use of for quick dispatch, are called so united in one subject, by one name; which by inadvertency we are apt to talk of and consider as one simple *Idea*, which indeed is a complication of many *Ideas* together.[1]

He later returns to the same topic, even more explicitly: 'These *Ideas* of Substances, though they are commonly called simple Apprehensions, and the names of them simple Terms; yet in effect are complex and compounded.'[2]

Why is it important for Locke that our ideas of substances are complex? The answer is one small part of a story too long to tell here. Briefly, however, Locke believes that we are doomed to conceive of natural species and genera in terms of lists of observable qualities and powers, commonly experienced in conjunction but, as far as we are concerned, otherwise unconnected. This experienced variety lies not in the object, but in the circumstances and our modes of sensibility. For we must suppose that it can in principle be explained by an underlying material structure affecting observers and surrounding objects in a variety of ways. That is why, included in the complex idea of the species, is the idea of an unknown substratum or subject of the observable qualities and powers, 'which Qualities', as Locke says, 'are commonly called Accidents'.[3] To know the thing itself would be to know its essence, but all we know are accidents.

This last claim is expressed in another well-known, but also much misunderstood passage, one which contains a clear allusion to traditional logical theory:

when we speak of any sort of Substance, we say it is a *thing* having such or such Qualities, as Body is a *thing* that is extended, figured, and capable

---

[1] *Essay*, II. xxiii. 1.   [2] *Essay*, II. xxiii. 14.
[3] *Essay*, II. xxiii. 2.

of Motion; a Spirit a *thing* capable of thinking; and so Hardness, Friability, and Power to draw Iron, we say, are Qualities to be found in a Loadstone. These, and the like fashions of speaking intimate, that the Substance is supposed always *something* besides the Extension, Figure, Solidity, Motion, Thinking, or other observable *Ideas*, though we know not what it is.[1]

It is paradigmatically accidents which, on Aristotelian theory, exist 'in' a subject. Locke is saying that our concept of the species is nothing but that of certain accidents in an otherwise unidentified substance: that is to say, the concept is compound.

Another part of Locke's argument denies the existence of objective specific essences at all. Although he has doubts about Boyle's version of mechanism, he is convinced that some mechanist theory is true. That means that the only essence or nature in the material world is the essence of matter itself, the nature from which flow the necessary laws of mechanics, whatever they may be. The particular species and genera, *horse*, *bird*, *gold*, *metal*, and so forth, are each, Locke thinks, arbitrarily distinguished by us through a defining set of observable attributes which he calls the 'nominal essence'. The only serious candidate for the 'real essence' of a species is that complex aspect of its unknown material structure which is responsible for the concurrence of those observable attributes by which the species is defined. There is nothing truly substantial or distinct or permanent about a 'real essence' so conceived. It exists as something distinct only relatively to the arbitrary nominal essence through which it is indirectly picked out.[2] All these doctrines are advanced in a complex but brilliantly effective and influential attack on the doctrine of predicables — 'this whole mystery of Genera and Species'[3] — which I have attempted to unravel elsewhere.[4] One small element in this attack is a point which is the obverse of the claim that our ideas of substances are complex: namely, that there is no ground for distinguishing an Aristotelian simple term, such as 'horse', from an Aristotelian compound term, such as 'palfrey', defined as a *horse which ambles*. It would therefore follow that the latter is logically as good a name of a species as the former, even if not so useful for the practising biologist.[5] The question how many species there are is for Locke the question how many names there are. Ice is a distinct species, he claims paradoxically, while molten gold

[1] *Essay*, II. xxiii. 3.   [2] Cf. *Essay*, III. vi. 6.
[3] *Essay*, III. iii. 9.
[4] 'Locke *versus* Aristotle on Natural Kinds', *Journal of Philosophy* (1981).
[5] Cf. *Essay*, IV. viii. 6.

is not, just because there is a distinct name for the former but not for the latter.[1] As he says in another allusion to Aristotelian theory, if we see something which falls outside our classification, we ask 'what it is, meaning by that Enquiry nothing but the Name'.[2]

For all that may be wrong with Aristotelian essences, these provocative contentions are today beyond belief, which may suggest that the truth lies somewhere between the two philosophies. For many reasons natural taxonomy, especially above the level of species, is a much more arbitrary business than the Aristotelian model allows. Yet Locke's solution, that it is a matter of entirely arbitrary, if informed, definition in terms of observable criteria fails to catch the semantic significance of the underlying affinity, whether evolutionary or structural, which is presumed to exist when items are placed in the same class. The issue is still an area of hot dispute in both biology and philosophical logic. As far as the latter is concerned, we still lack an agreed and convincing account of the significance of the Aristotelian distinction between what is simple and what is composite, and will no doubt continue to do so until we have a better theory of the relation between individual and species. What is certain is that the distinction cannot be safely ignored.

Locke's inclusion of the ideas of body and spirit among his examples of complex ideas of substances indicates that he was fighting on two fronts, bearing Descartes in mind even in the act of challenging Aristotelian substantial forms. Descartes, however, stands clear of traditional logic in a number of ways. In particular, the distinction between terms and propositions is irrelevant to his conception of simple and complex. His notion of a simple idea itself embraces what is propositional. One reason for this somewhat unorthodox approach to thought must lie in his famous theory of judgement. On the current Aristotelian doctrine, as we have seen, 'judgement' or mental 'affirmation' was the act of combining 'simple apprehensions'. Such terminology conflates propositional thought with acceptance or belief, a definite propositional attitude. Yet Descartes holds that assent to a proposition is voluntary, an act of will which comes after the work of the understanding. For him, whatever can be believed can be held in mind or 'perceived' prior to acceptance, rejection, or suspense of judgement. By this two-stage model he explains error, which is supposed to occur only when we judge rashly in the absence of

[1] *Essay*, IV. vi. 13.   [2] *Essay*, II. xxxii. 7.

clear and distinct perceptions or ideas. The term 'idea' therefore covers whatever is an object of the understanding antecedently to assent or dissent. An 'idea' is typically what Descartes calls 'material' for a belief. He does say that an idea is not capable of truth or falsity in the strict sense, but that is only because he regards beliefs as the primary bearers of truth and falsity, while ideas can occur within the context of other mental states such as desire. It is not because ideas are never propositional in form. Accordingly ideas can be said to be 'materially' true or false, in whatever context they occur.[1]

There are other considerations which may help to explain Descartes's approach. He holds that every conscious state or act involves an idea, and that every idea is an idea *of* something. That is to say, an idea is essentially referred or related to an object, and such reference seems to be interpreted as itself a kind of propositional thought.[2] Another motive may be supplied by the point that to have a Cartesian clear and distinct idea of something is to understand it. It is difficult to separate our understanding, for example, what identity is, from our grasping such principles as that, if A is identical with B and B with C, then A is identical with C. That particular principle is, as it happens, included explicitly in Descartes's sample list of 'simple notions'.[3]

All this seems to have set a problem for Descartes's followers, for Aristotelian logic was too impressive and too prestigious simply to be jettisoned. Besides, empiricists like Hobbes and Gassendi were already incorporating it into their systems with some popular success. Arnauld's solution, in what was to become the standard Cartesian logic, takes the bull by the horns. The Cartesian distinction between perception and assent, the understanding and the will, is in effect identified with the distinction between the simple apprehension of the meaning of terms and the mental affirmation of propositions. As on the traditional account, a propositional content comes into existence only with a propositional attitude. Elsewhere Arnauld is ready to deal with the content of wishes and other non-cognitive states of mind simply by postulating other sorts of combinatory act than judgements.[4] The traditional conception of combination was, then, securely re-established by the time Locke began to write, despite what may seem the obvious objection that, as Thomas Reid was to put it,

---

[1] Cf. *Meditations*, III (with Descartes's reply to Arnauld's objections) and IV.

[2] Cf. *Passions of the Soul*, I. 22–5.

[3] *Rules for the Direction of the Mind*, xii.

[4] A. Arnauld and C. Lancelot, *A General and Rational Grammar* (1662), I. ii. 4. Cf. Port-Royal *Logic*, Introduction; II. iii.

'it is one thing to conceive the meaning of a proposition; it is another thing to judge it to be true or false'.[1] For Locke 'perception' and 'judgement' are acts of propositional composition and it is for that reason that he calls ideas the 'materials' of knowledge and belief. It is not because they constitute, as Descartes holds, propositional material for assent.

One line of approach to Descartes's employment of the notion of simplicity is to see him less as the questing philosopher of popular imagination, endeavouring as best he can to escape from scepticism to certainty by some rigorous linear argument, than as a philosopher struck by the need to explain what he takes to be our—especially his own—remarkable capacity for knowledge. For Descartes was convinced that all material change is in accordance with simple and necessary mechanical laws; and that, with the aid of some theological bolstering, these laws can be derived *a priori* from a suitably refined understanding of what it is to be material, that is, from the intelligible essence of matter.[2] He supposed that the intellect can penetrate—that his own intellect had penetrated—to the hidden principles of things. But how could such a thing be done? The problem is like Kant's problem—How is synthetic *a priori* knowledge possible?—but Descartes saw nothing wrong with a metaphysical answer. The intellect can spin knowledge from its own entrails because God created it with the means to do so. We have innate ideas, capacities for knowledge of fundamental principles which can be made explicit if we adopt the proper method.

A first principle of Descartes's method is that what is complex and not understood should be broken down into what is simple and intelligible and evidently true.[3] These simple ideas, as Spinoza tells us in his exposition of Descartes, must be examined individually: 'For if he could perceive simple ideas clearly and distinctly, he would doubtless understand all the other ideas composed of those simple ones, with the same clarity and perspicuity.'[4] Analysis is to be followed by synthesis.[5] The theory is full of Aristotelian overtones. The Aristotelian principle that what is uncombined is incapable of either truth or falsity is retained as the principle that only what is complex can be false. 'Simple natures', we are told, 'are known *per se* and are wholly free from

---

[1] *Essays on the Intellectual Powers of Man* (1785), I. i. 8.
[2] Cf. *Principles of Philosophy*, II. 36–44.
[3] Cf. *Rules*, v–vi.
[4] Spinoza, *Principles of Cartesian Philosophy* (1663), introduction.
[5] Cf. *Rules*, xiii.

falsity.' There is nothing in a simple nature not completely known because 'otherwise it could not be called simple, but must be complex—a compound of the element we perceive and the supposed unknown element'.[1] As the Aristotelian stripped away accidents to leave bare the essence and properties of the species, Descartes strips inessentials from our everyday conception of a body to reveal the simple idea of extension and other simple ideas, such as mobility and duration, which are necessarily connected to extension. The simplicity and intelligibility of these ideas is for him a kind of guarantee, through the goodness of God, that they are 'true' and pertain to reality. They constitute a dependable link between the subjective realm of ideas and what is objective and external.

Locke's epistemology is the antithesis of all this, but is expressed in remarkably similar terms. The link with reality is not innate and intellectual but adventitious and sensory. He states the problem very explicitly, like Descartes, in the form of a hypothetical scepticism:

> 'Tis evident, the Mind knows not Things immediately, but only by the intervention of the *Ideas* it has of them. *Our knowledge* therefore is *real*, only so far as there is a conformity between our *Ideas* and the reality of Things. But what shall be here the Criterion? How shall the Mind, when it perceives nothing but its own *Ideas*, know that they agree with Things themselves?[2]

But the question is not put in any spirit of perplexity, as many critics have assumed. It is simply the prelude to a summary statement of Locke's clear, confident, highly theoretical and deliberately anti-Cartesian answer to it. That answer, like Descartes's, hinges on the distinction between simple and complex ideas. It also hinges on a neat causal theory of representation.

Simple ideas, as we know, are necessarily received through the senses or reflection. That is to say (to ignore the special case of 'reflection'), they are caused in us by external things acting on the senses. For that very reason simple ideas must be taken to correspond to their objects in regular and orderly ways, even if we do not know the nature of those objects or how they act on us. A simple idea is therefore a natural sign of its cause. It is naturally fitted to represent in thought that attribute of reality, whatever it may be, which is in general responsible for our receiving ideas or sensations of that type.[3] Thus the simple idea or appearance of

---

[1] *Rules*, xii.   [2] *Essay*, iv. iv. 3.
[3] Cf. *Essay*, iv. xi. 2.

white received in sensation and capable of being recalled in the imagination represents in thought whatever in the object underlies its general disposition or power regularly to cause just that sensation in us. This power Locke calls the 'quality' of the object.

It follows that simple ideas are all necessarily 'real' and 'conform' to things. They cannot be 'fantastical':

simple Ideas *are not fictions* of our Fancies, but the natural and regular productions of Things without us, really operating upon us; and so carry with them all the conformity which is intended . . . Thus the *Idea* of Whiteness, or Bitterness, as it is in the Mind, exactly answering that Power which is in any Body to produce it there, has all the real conformity it can, or ought to have, with Things without us.[1]

Similar arguments go to prove that simple ideas are necessarily adequate and also 'true', in the loose sense in which ideas can be said to be true if something exists conforming to them.[2] For Locke as for Descartes, falsity and inadequacy only arise when there is complexity.

It is significant that the very ideas which for Locke epitomize simplicity, ideas of colours, were taken by Cartesians to exemplify composition. Descartes took the ordinary idea of a colour to include both the bare image or sensation and an 'obscure judgement' as to its unknown cause. Two other sorts of ideas of a colour are possible: first, the rash and false idea which incorporates the judgement that the cause of the sensation is qualitatively like the sensation, that the sensation of colour represents its cause as it is in the object; and, secondly, the clear and distinct, materially true idea which refers the sensation to mechanical causes in the object.[3] All, however, are complex. For Locke, on the other hand, the sensation or image *is* the idea, and his criterion for its simplicity is phenomenal, the limits of phenomenal discrimination. Each simple idea, being 'in it self uncompounded, contains in it nothing but *one uniform Appearance*'.[4] This simple appearance *represents* something, but the causal relation which constitutes the representative relation does not enter into the content of the idea, as it does for Descartes. Still less do speculations as to the intrinsic nature of the unknown cause: simple ideas do not, Locke tells us, 'become liable to any Imputation of *Falshood*, if the Mind (as in most Men I believe it

[1] *Essay*, IV. iv. 4. Cf. II. xxx. 2.
[2] Cf. *Essay*, II. xxxi. 2; II. xxxii. 14.
[3] Cf. *Principles*, I. 66–73; *Meditations*, III and VI. Cf., too, Arnauld, *Logic*, I. ix.
[4] *Essay*, II. ii. 1.

does) judges these Ideas to be in the Things themselves'.[1] For they are 'as real distinguishing Characters, whether they be only constant Effects, or else exact Resemblances of something in the things themselves'.[2] With phenomenal simplicity goes indefinability, for the idea of a colour, like any simple idea, cannot be conveyed in words. This familiar point was taken by Leibniz, but he remains obdurately Cartesian. Five years before the publication of the *Essay*, he had written,

> we are not able to explain to the blind what red is; nor can we make manifest to others any object of this kind except by bringing the thing before them, so that they may be made to see, smell or taste the same; . . . It is nevertheless certain that these notions are composite, and may be resolved, since they have their several causes.[3]

Despite this disagreement over paradigms, there are some ideas which are simple for both Locke and Descartes: for example, very general ideas like *existence* and *unity* which figure in Cartesian 'eternal truths'. For Locke, however, such ideas are mere abstractions from experience, and there are no eternal truths outside our own minds. A different problem is raised by the question, 'What are the simple ideas of extension?' Here Locke is pulled in two directions. He sees the claims to be simple of the general or determinable concept, which any Cartesian would have chosen, but he unsurprisingly prefers what he calls 'a sensible Point', 'the least portion of Space or Extension, whereof we have a clear and distinct *Idea*'. As he recognizes, his paradigms do not fit extension very neatly, but he is no more in real retreat than Leibniz was over colours. As a footnote to the Fifth Edition of the *Essay* reports him, '. . . if the *Idea* of Extension is so peculiar, that it cannot exactly agree with the Definition that he has given of those *Simple Ideas*, so that it differs in some manner from all others of that kind, he thinks 'tis better to leave it there expos'd to this Difficulty, than to make a new Division in his Favour. 'Tis enough for Mr. *Locke* that his Meaning can be understood.' The objection is dismissed as a pedantic nicety which does not touch the real issues.[4]

We can say, then, that a fundamental difference of view over the nature of what ties thought to reality—innate structural interpretive principles versus reliable experiential building-blocks—found expression within the general framework of a

[1] *Essay*, II. xxxii. 14.
[2] *Essay*, II. xxx. 2.
[3] Leibniz, 'Reflections on Knowledge, Truth and Ideas' (1684).
[4] *Essay*, II. xv. 9, with footnote in 5th edn.

compositionalist theory of ideas.[1] Unless we recognize that relationship and the methodological and epistemological point of Locke's variety of compositionalism, it is easy to exaggerate both the limitations which it placed on his thought and apparent inconsistencies in his argument. In a notorious passage he seems ready to allow that, after all, no idea whatsoever enjoys absolute simplicity, since all ideas, 'when attentively considered', include 'some kind of relation' in them. 'And sensible Qualities,' he asks, 'what are they but the Powers of different Bodies, in relation to our Perception . . . And if considered in the things themselves, do they not depend on the Bulk, Figure, Texture, and Motion of the Parts?'[2] Yet the point is not an abject capitulation to the Cartesian conception of the complex idea of a sensible quality, nor is it an even more abject flight from compositionalism altogether. It is part of an argument for including ideas of powers in the class of simple ideas, by contrast with ideas of substances. Locke has in mind that ideas of substances may be formed more or less well and appropriately and carefully, whereas our idea of the power of a thing, say the power of wax to be melted by gentle heat, an idea which we acquire when we take note of its regular observable behaviour, leaves, so Locke thought, no comparable room for error. The appearance of the regular effect adequately 'represents' a power both in the agent, the source of heat, and in the patient, the wax. In other words, it represents whatever in each object underlies or causes the observed tendency, just as the idea of white adequately represents whatever in the object regularly causes that idea in us. No mere analytical method applied to our ideas will take us further in either case, for our knowledge and thought about the world stands on such 'simple' representative relationships, founded on experience. It is this epistemological simplicity which really counts as simplicity in Locke's eyes.

What, then, is the role of analysis for Locke? I can give only a rough and partial answer now. Like Descartes, he recommends that we examine our complex ideas part by part as a route to what he calls 'clear and distinct' ideas. Yet this Cartesian phrase has been radically reinterpreted in line with Locke's conviction that no method will enable us to penetrate with certainty and full understanding beyond the limits of observation. We are condemned to speculative hypothesis employing only experiential concepts. One thing method can do, however, is to keep us pressed

[1] The possibility of such a comparison is briefly mentioned, but not explored, by Gibson, op. cit., p. 48.

[2] *Essay*, II. xxi. 3.

up against this barrier by eliminating mere unclarity of thought. Here the impediment is not a veil of ideas so much as a veil of words which can entangle and impose on us especially with respect to the formation of complex ideas. To overcome this impediment we need a systematic, settled, and public way of thinking about nature and human affairs: that is to say, orderly and settled systems of complex ideas and an orderly and settled vocabulary to express them. Ordinary or 'civil' language is for various reasons inadequate, and a strict or 'philosophical' language needs to be introduced. Locke is here acting as spokesman for the programme of linguistic reform, especially in chemical and biological classification, initiated by Bacon's denunciation of the 'Idols of the Market-place' and taken up by the Royal Society. This programme, in Locke's eyes, concerns complex ideas. For simple ideas, just as they are necessarily 'adequate' and 'true' in their relation to reality, so are they almost inevitably, even if not necessarily, 'clear and distinct' and all that is good in their relation to a public language.[1] That is to say, problems of meaning and communication can arise (or arose in the seventeenth century, in Locke's reasonable view) when men talk and think in chemistry of 'liquor', 'salt', or 'metal', in biology of 'fish' or 'shrubs', and in ethics of 'honour' or 'justice', but they do not in general arise in respect of such simpler predicates as 'blue' or 'square'. The chief remedy for such problems, therefore, to which Locke devotes a significant part of the *Essay*, consists in the analysis of the complex into the simple.

There are many gaps in the present argument,[2] but I have tried to give at least an impression of the depth and complexity of the context which supplied Locke both with the tool of compositionalism and with the problems on which he brought it to bear. In studying such relationships between thinker and context I believe that we are studying human rationality itself. Perhaps what is chiefly wrong with the proposal that Locke adopted compositionalism in emulation of physical theory is that it grossly underestimates that rationality in his case.

[1] Cf. *Essay*, II. xxix. 7; III. iv. 15.
[2] I have discussed only certain Lockean simple and complex ideas, and I have not considered how much Locke owes, e.g., to Hobbes or Gassendi.

LOCKE AND THE ETHICS OF BELIEF

By J. A. PASSMORE

I PROPOSE to look critically at Locke's answer to three closely related questions:

1. Are there any circumstances whatsoever in which we can properly be described as 'choosing', or 'deciding', whether or not to believe p?

2. If there are such circumstances, does our decision to believe p rather than to disbelieve it ever make us liable to moral censure?

3. If there are no such circumstances, are there any other circumstances in which we can properly be praised or blamed for believing p?

If I have chosen to subject Locke, in particular, to such a triune inquisition this is for three reasons. First, because his discussion of these questions is lengthy, detailed, and honest; secondly, because it has been very little explored by Locke scholars; thirdly, because on the face of it Locke falls into puzzling inconsistencies, which need some sort of explanation.

To begin from the last point. A passage in Locke's *A Letter on Toleration* lays it down quite explicitly that 'to believe this or that to be true is not within the scope of our will'.[1] And, as we shall see, this is by no means the only occasion on which he so definitely denies that men can ever choose what they shall believe. Yet no less explicitly, this time in his *Essay concerning Human Understanding*, he distinguishes a class of cases in which 'Assent, Suspense, or Dissent, are often voluntary Actions' (XX. 15)[2]. ('Belief', one should note, he identifies with assent.) Throughout his account of belief, furthermore, Locke relies upon that doctrine which he sums up in one of his running

---

[1] *Letter on Toleration*, ed. R. Klibansky (Oxford, 1968), Eng. trans. J. W. Gough, p. 121. The original latin reads: 'Ut hoc vel illud verum esse credamus, in nostra voluntate situm non est.'

[2] All quotations from the *Essay* are as in John Locke, *An Essay Concerning Human Understanding*, ed. P. H. Nidditch (Oxford, 1975). Nidditch's copy text is the fourth edition. Since most references are to Bk. IV, I cite only, in such cases, the chapter and section.

heads: 'Our Assent ought to be regulated by the grounds of Probability' (XVI. 1). Assuming only that 'ought' implies 'can', that 'ought' means something stronger than 'it would be nice if', the Utopian sense of 'ought' in which we might tell someone that he ought to be President of the United States, this appears to entail that we are free thus to regulate, or not to regulate, our assent. Indeed, Locke's main contribution to philosophy, so Gilbert Ryle has somewhat narrowly but not absurdly argued, consists in his having shown us that 'the tenacity with which people hold their opinions is not always, but ought always, to be proportioned to the quantity and quality of the reasons which can be adduced for them'.[1] And 'ought always to be proportioned' seems to commit Locke to something like W. K. Clifford's main thesis in 'The Ethics of Belief': 'It is wrong always, everywhere, and for anyone, to believe anything upon insufficient evidence'.[2] (Although Ryle, we note with interest, ascribes to Locke not 'an ethics of belief' but an 'ethics of thinking'.)

I said that Locke's views had been neglected. Although it presents us with such striking problems in interpretation, the penultimate segment of the *Essay* (XIX–XX) in which Locke presents his theory, or his theories, on belief, has never been, so far as I know, closely studied. Aaron takes the view that Locke was tiring of his task when he came near to its end, and offers in evidence the fact that he did not revise these chapters as closely as he did their predecessors.[3] Admittedly, they contain an exceptional degree of repetition, a common sign of fatigue. Yet they are quite fundamental for Locke. There were two projects particularly dear to his heart: the first, to advocate, if only within limits, religious toleration; the second, to undermine one particular sort of religion, 'enthusiasm', fanaticism, yet without weakening religious faith. The epistemological foundations of his argument are, in both cases, expounded in these chapters. He did not revise them, one might plausibly suggest, not because he was tired but because the ideas they contain were so fundamental to his thinking, not revisable; the repetitions arise from his determination to hammer home the crucial points.

[1] Gilbert Ryle, 'John Locke', first delivered as a lecture in 1965, reprinted in *Collected Papers* (London, 1971), vol. i; the passage quoted is on p. 156.

[2] First published in *Contemporary Review*, Jan. 1877, reprinted in Leslie Stephen and Frederick Pollock, *The Ethics of Belief and Other Essays* (London, 1947). The passage quoted is on p. 77.

[3] Richard Aaron, *John Locke*, 3rd edn. (Oxford, 1971), p. 248.

(He added to the fourth edition, indeed, a new chapter 'Of Enthusiasm', still further to insist upon them.)

To turn now to the detail and the honesty of Locke's argument, let us look first at the definition of belief which he offers us: 'the admitting or receiving any Proposition for true, upon Arguments or Proofs that are found to persuade us to receive it as true, without certain Knowledge that it is so' (XV. 3). Believing, it will be plain, is on this view an imperfect surrogate for knowing, made necessary, Locke tells us, by the fact that true knowledge is 'very short and scanty' (XIV. 1). When immediate intuition does not suffice, demonstration can give us knowledge; we *see* that the conclusion of the demonstration must be true. But where such demonstrations are lacking, as they mostly are, we have no option but to fall back upon probable reasoning. Notice that on Locke's definition there is no such thing as an entirely groundless belief; we are persuaded by 'Arguments or Proofs' to accept as true those propositions we believe to be true. This is so, even although the 'proofs' do not amount to demonstrations. Locke defines belief, then, as a purely intellectual operation, in a way which emphasizes at once its likeness, and its inferiority, to knowledge.

It is not at all surprising, in the light of this definition, that Locke generally prefers to speak in terms of 'assent' rather than of 'belief', even although, as we said, he takes them to be synonymous. The mere having of an idea as the result of experience does not for Locke, as it does for Hume, count as believing.[1] We 'believe' only when a proposition is before us for our consideration and there are 'inducements' for us to accept it as true—grounds, that is, which make it seem probable, likely to be true. These 'inducements' may be of either of two sorts, the conformity of the proposition with 'our own Knowledge, Observation and Experience' or 'the Testimony of others, vouching their Observation and Experience'.

The two grounds of probability will, in favourable circumstances, reinforce one another. '[A]s the conformity of our Knowledge, as the certainty of Observations, as the frequency and constancy of Experience, and the number and credibility of Testimonies, do more or less agree, or disagree with it, so is any Proposition in it self, more or less probable' (XV. 6). Many people, Locke confesses, give assent to propositions on much weaker grounds than this; they assent to propositions, indeed,

[1] Compare J. A. Passmore, 'Hume and the Ethics of Belief' in G. P. Morice (ed.), *David Hume: Bicentenary Papers* (Edinburgh, 1977), pp. 77–92.

merely because someone tells them that they are true. But this is a 'wrong ground of Assent'; those who have recourse to it are not proceeding rationally.

The Mind if it will proceed rationally, ought to examine all the grounds of Probability, and see how they make more or less, *for or against* any probable Proposition, before it assents to or dissents from it, and upon a due balancing the whole, reject, or receive it, with a more or less firm assent, proportionably to the preponderancy of the greater grounds of Probability on the one side or the other [XV. 5].

On the assumption that for Locke belief is involuntary, his choice of language in this analysis of belief and probability may somewhat surprise us. When we believe, he has said, we 'admit' propositions as true, we 'receive' them as such. As the *Oxford English Dictionary* explicitly points out, the primary use of the word 'admit' is voluntary. We can admit, or we can refuse to admit, a person to our house; we can admit, or we can refuse to admit, to a fault, to a responsibility, or that something is the case. The word 'receive' is more often involuntary in its connotations. But when, as here, it is linked with 'admit', it is natural to read it as having that sense in which a person 'receives callers' or 'receives guests' or 'receives stolen goods'—in each case a voluntary act. A 'received opinion', we might add in favour of this interpretation, is surely an opinion which is generally *accepted*. And 'accepting' is, in most contexts, something we choose to do.

Coupling Locke's analysis of the way in which the beliefs of a rational man are founded on the probabilities with his use of such words as 'admitting' and 'receiving' to describe our coming to believe, we should very naturally interpret his analysis of rational belief in something like the following manner: a proposition is put before us, or we put it before ourselves, for our consideration; we estimate its probability in the light of the arguments for and against its being true; we give our assent to it with a degree of assurance proportionate to its relative probability. But this analysis is precisely parallel to the analysis we should offer if we were asked to give an account of what we mean by a rational *decision*. A proposed course of action, we might then say, is put before us, or we put it before ourselves, for our consideration; we estimate its desirability in the light of the considerations for and against it; we agree to it if the considerations *pro* are stronger than the considerations *contra*. So on this interpretation belief would simply be one form of decision-making, that form in which the considerations *pro* and *contra* are considerations of probability. And if such decision-making is not voluntary, then what *is* voluntary? The only question which could remain is whether irrational belief is also voluntary. Yet Locke, as we saw, asserts all belief to be involuntary, whether it be rational or irrational.

Faced with so absolute a contradiction between what seems to be entailed—viz. that belief is one form of voluntary decision—by the interpretation we have so far favoured and the doctrine to which Locke so firmly commits himself, that belief is *not* a voluntary decision, we have no option but to look again at our interpretation. Then we notice that even although Locke certainly tells us that a man must *if he will proceed rationally* assent to a proposition with a degree of assurance proportional to its probability, where the phrase 'if he will proceed rationally' would suggest that irrational people do not thus regulate their assent, he also tells us that no one, rational or irrational, can help giving his assent to the more probable proposition. The probability, for Locke as not for Hume, is one thing, the degree of assurance another, but the first necessarily engenders the second. '[T]hat a Man should afford his Assent to that side, on which the less Probability appears to him, seems to me utterly impracticable, and as impossible, as it is to believe the same thing probable and improbable at the same time' (XX. 15). If we take this to be Locke's considered opinion, two conclusions seem to follow. The first, that where we went wrong in our previous analysis of Locke's argument was in supposing that after considering the *pro* and *contra* probabilities a person, on Locke's view, *decides* to believe or not to believe. No such decision, it would now appear, enters into the situation. Finding the probabilities *pro* a proposition to be more powerful than the consideration *contra* that proposition, a person cannot but believe the proposition with a degree of assurance proportional to the degree to which it seems to him to be more probable. There is no choice in the matter. The second conclusion is that when Locke tells us that 'our Assent ought to be regulated by the grounds of Probability', i.e. the actual or real grounds of probability, he must after all be using 'ought' in its Utopian sense, must be saying that the world would be a better place if people so regulated their assent, rather than that they are under a moral obligation to do so. And Ryle, too, must be using 'ought' in this Utopian sense when he sums up Locke's conclusion in the maxim that 'the tenacity with which people hold their opinions is not always, but ought always, to be proportioned to the quantity and quality of the reasons which can be adduced for them'. No doubt, in an ideal world assent would be governed by *the* grounds of probability, by the reasons which *can* be adduced. But in any actual world human beings will believe not in accordance with the grounds which *can* be adduced but in accordance with the grounds they actually have before them, however feeble they may be; they will automatically give their assent to what seems to them, at that moment, the most probable view. To tell them that they ought to believe in accordance with the *real* probabilities, the grounds that *can* be adduced, as distinct from the immediately obvious probabilities, is to tell them they ought to do what they cannot possibly do. 'Admit' and 'receive' have, on this showing, their passive sense, that passive sense in which wax admits, or receives, impressions. Does not Locke tell us that the mind is like a piece of wax? A 'received opinion' is not, it would seem, an opinion we have accepted—for the concept of 'acceptance' is irremediably voluntary—but rather an opinion which has impressed itself upon us.

But setting out to avoid an interpretation of Locke which led inevitably to the conclusion that belief was a voluntary decision we have now substituted an analysis which Locke would find quite as unpalatable, with its consequence that no one can ever be blamed for believing as he does, since we believe as we must. As a defender of toleration, to be sure, Locke might find this conclusion palatable but not as a critic of enthusiasm. He wants to be able to blame the enthusiast, as indeed the atheist, for believing as he does.

Perhaps there is a way out. We distinguished two senses of the phrase 'grounds of Assent'—the sense in which it means the *real* grounds as they would be known to an ideal human observer, the Utopian grounds, and the sense in which it means the grounds as an agent immediately perceives them. But when Locke talks about 'the grounds of Assent' or 'the real grounds' or, in Ryle's phrase, 'the reasons which can be adduced', he usually means something which falls between these two extremes. He means the grounds, the reasons, which would be available to us if we chose to inquire, the reasons which somebody—not an ideal observer, but someone who has investigated further than we have done—would be in a position to put before us, or which we ourselves could discover, if we inquired further. It is *these* grounds, we might now suggest, which ought, on Locke's view, to regulate our assent. We can be blamed for not regulating the degree of our assent by reference to them, just because we can be blamed for not carrying our inquiries as far as we should have done.

Such an interpretation, one might continue by arguing, would square with Locke's attempt, towards the very end of his *Essay* (XX. 16), to draw a parallel, in respect to the character and limits of their involuntariness, between belief, perception, and knowledge. To see the point of this parallel, we shall have to revert to an earlier chapter (XIII) in which Locke attempts to establish the involuntariness of perception and knowledge while yet leaving open a very restricted sense in which they are voluntary. It in no way depends on a perceiver's will, Locke there says, whether he sees something as black or yellow, whether he feels it as cold or as scalding hot. 'The Earth will not appear painted with Flowers, nor the Fields covered with Verdure, whenever he has a Mind to it: in the cold Winter, he cannot help seeing it white and hoary, if he will look abroad' (XIII. 2). We are free, in respect to perception, only this far; we are free to decide whether to inspect such a landscape more closely 'and with an intent application, endeavour to observe accurately all that is visible in it' or, on the contrary, simply to take it in at a glance and pass on to other matters.

Similarly with knowledge. In respect to its voluntariness as in so many other respects, 'knowledge', Locke argues, 'has a great Conformity with our Sight'. Like perception, it is *neither wholly necessary nor wholly voluntary*. Just as, if only we open our eyes, we cannot help seeing the winter landscape as white, so too, if we choose to compare our ideas, we cannot but see that they are related in particular ways, and thus arrive at knowledge. Given only that we have the concepts of one, two, three, and six we see at once, if we take the trouble to compare them, that, taken together, one, two, and three make six. Given, too, that we compare the concepts of frail dependent man and omnipotent God we cannot but see that 'Man is to honour, fear, and obey GOD'. But if we do not choose to compare our ideas, this knowledge, mathematical or moral, will never come our way.

[A]ll that is *voluntary* in our Knowledge [so Locke sums up], is the *employing*, or with-holding any of *our Faculties* from this or that sort of Objects, and a more, or less accurate survey of them: But they being employed, *our Will hath no Power to determine the Knowledge of the Mind* one way or other; that is done only by the Objects themselves, as far as they are clearly discovered [XIII. 2].

What we have before our minds, that is, determines what we know. Our knowledge is voluntary only in so far as we can decide what we *do* have before our minds.

Now for the comparison with belief.

> As Knowledge, is no more arbitrary than Perception [Locke writes], so, I think, Assent is no more in our Power than Knowledge. When the Agreement of any two *Ideas* appears to our Minds, whether immediately, or by the Assistance of Reason, I can no more refuse to perceive, no more avoid knowing it, than I can avoid seeing those Objects, which I turn my Eyes to, and look on in day-light: And what upon full Examination I find the most probable, I cannot deny my Assent to. . . . Yet *we can hinder both Knowledge and Assent, by stopping our Enquiry*, and not imploying our Faculties in the search of any Truth. If it were not so, Ignorance, Error, or Infidelity could not in any Case be a Fault. Thus in some Cases, we can prevent or suspend our Assent: But can a Man, versed in modern or ancient History, doubt whether there be such a Place as *Rome*, or whether there was such a Man as *Julius Caesar*? [XX. 16].

Notice the progress of Locke's argument, which is consistent with our initial assumptions about his intentions. He is far from denying that ignorance, error, and infidelity can in some circumstances be a fault. ('Infidelity', of course, in that sense which links it with 'being an infidel', with disbelieving.) The enthusiast and the atheist can be condemned on moral grounds, for believing what they should not believe. The only problem, as he sees it, is to reconcile this undoubted truth with his other, no less firm, conviction that belief is never, in the full sense, voluntary.

He tries to reconcile his two basic convictions by applying to the case of belief what he had previously said about perception and knowledge. In the same sense in which we cannot help perceiving that the landscape before our eyes is white, or knowing that two and two make four, we cannot help believing that there is such a city as Rome and that there was such a person as Julius Caesar. But just as it lies within our power to decide whether merely to glance at the snow or to look at it closely, to study or not to study arithmetic, so too, he argues, it lies in our power to decide whether to scrutinize a proposition carefully before we assent to it. Only so far is belief voluntary.

It would seem, then, that Locke gives a clear and definite answer to each of our original three questions. There are *no* circumstances in which we decide to believe *p*; the question whether we can be blamed for thus deciding does not, therefore, ever arise. Nevertheless, there are circumstances in which we can be blamed for believing *p*. This is when we believe *p* without having sufficiently explored the possibility that it is false and if we had done so would have disbelieved it.

Not, Locke now hastens to add, that it is always our duty to inquire before we believe. We are not called upon to submit *all* our beliefs to critical investigation. Precepts so rigorous as this would place an intolerable burden on us. In a great many cases it is a matter of no consequence, whether to ourselves or to other people, what we believe—'whether our King *Richard* the Third was crook-back'd, or no; or whether *Roger Bacon* was a Mathematician, or a Magician'. In such instances ''tis not strange, that the Mind should give it self up to the common Opinion, or render it self to the first Comer'—not strange, and perfectly forgiveable. We do not decide to believe such propositions; we simply acquiesce in them without inquiry. He suggests, even, that in respect to such opinions we are free; 'the Mind lets them float at liberty'. This is not merely a loose metaphor. For he continues thus: 'where the Mind judges that the Proposition has concernment in it . . . and the Mind sets it self seriously to enquire, and examine the Probability: there, I think, it is not in our Choice, to take which side we please, if manifest odds appear on either. The greater Probability, I think, in that Case, will determine the Assent' (XX. 16). So Locke is drawing a contrast. He is arguing that it is only when we inquire closely that we are not free to choose—'*there*, it is not in our Choice, to take which side we please'; 'the greater probability will *in that Case* determine the Assent'. He is leaving open the possibility, which he had previously rejected, of our 'taking what side we please'—if only in respect to unimportant beliefs into the grounds of which we have not deeply inquired.

We can, however, save Locke's central doctrine that belief is involuntary, even if at the cost of this contrast, by withdrawing his concession that in the case of the floating opinion we are free to choose what to believe. Such an opinion, he might have said, simply enters our mind and lodges there. He himself compares it, indeed, with a mote entering our eye. But in that case he will have to modify his earlier definition of belief. For these will then be *groundless* beliefs. Perhaps we should rather suggest, as being Locke's central view, that such beliefs are accepted by us on the ground that they are commonly asserted. What Locke is really telling us, on this view, is that only if we inquire will our beliefs be regulated by real probabilities, as distinct from such 'wrong grounds of Assent' as popular opinion.

One now begins to understand why Ryle ascribed to Locke an 'ethics of thinking' rather than an 'ethics of belief'. For where we go wrong, on this interpretation, is in failing to investigate rather than in believing or failing to believe. Our investigations, Locke freely admits, may in some cases lead us astray. As a result of investigating, we may arrive at a false belief which, had we not investigated, would never have occurred to us. But that does not mean that we were then wrong to investigate. 'He that examines, and upon a fair examination embraces an error for a truth', he writes in a *Commonplace Book* entry, 'has done his duty', the 'duty to search after truth'.[1]

If we accept this interpretation, then we could put Locke's argument thus: 'Just as what we know depends on what ideas we have before us, so what we believe depends on what *evidence* we have before us. But it is often the case that we would have had different evidence before us had we investigated further. When the question at issue is one of great importance we ought therefore to investigate it further. So to say that our beliefs *ought* to be regulated by the grounds of probability—that these grounds are not only "the Foundations on which our *Assent* is built" but also "the measure whereby its several degrees are, or ought to be, *regulated*" (XVI. 1)—means that although the evidence we at any time have before us will *in fact* determine the degree of our assent, yet our degree of assent *ought* to be regulated by the evidence we *would* have had before us had we chosen to inquire.'

Clearly, however, something has now gone seriously wrong, at least on the assumption that 'ought' implies 'can'. If our degree of assurance is inevitably determined by the evidence we have before us, if belief is simply something we passively have in the presence of such evidence, just as the perception of a snowy landscape is something we passively have, on Locke's view, in the presence of such a landscape, what is the point of telling us that we ought not to believe until we inquire further? It would certainly be quite ridiculous to say that we ought not to perceive the landscape until we have examined it more closely. Remember Locke's definition of rational procedure: '*the Mind . . . ought to examine all the grounds of Probability*, and see how they make more or less, *for or against* any probable Proposition, before it assents to or dissents from it' (XVI. 5).

---

[1] 'Error' in Lord King, *The Life of John Locke* (2nd edn. London, 1830), ii, 75 f.

This *simply isn't possible*, if we automatically respond with the appropriate degree of assurance to any proposition as soon as we have it before us.

Once more, our attempt to interpret Locke seems to have reached an impasse. Perhaps we had better look again at the alleged parallelism between belief and knowledge in case that is what has been misleading us. In the course of drawing this parallel, Locke tells us that we can 'suspend or prevent' our belief. And this is exactly what he must be urging us to do, when he lays it down that our beliefs ought to be regulated by the evidence we *could* have had before us had we investigated rather than by the evidence we have before us prior to investigation. For this implies that we can stop ourselves from believing until we have conducted these investigations. What corresponds to such suspension or prevention in the case of knowledge? Locke's answer is clear enough: '*we can hinder both Knowledge and Assent by stopping our Enquiry.*' We can prevent ourselves from knowing any geometry by not studying it, we can suspend our knowledge of geometry by ceasing to study it. Similarly, then, we can prevent ourselves from believing that Caesar was assassinated by not studying ancient history and suspend any further beliefs about his assassination by ceasing to read as soon as we discover that he was assassinated. But that is not at all what Locke has in mind when he grants that we can sometimes suspend our belief. Neither is it what we ordinarily have in mind when we use that phrase. (Incidentally, we never speak of ourselves as 'suspending our knowledge'.)

Suppose, for example, I go to see a play about the assassination of Julius Caesar. I may wonder whether it gives an accurate account of the assassination. I describe myself as 'suspending' my belief that it does, or does not, until I can inquire further, perhaps by reading a history textbook when I return home. (This is not at all the same thing, I should perhaps add, as the Coleridgian 'willing suspension of disbelief'.) 'Suspending my belief' is by no means equivalent, then, to ceasing to inquire. Rather, I suspend my belief until I *can* inquire, perhaps because I previously knew nothing about Julius Caesar but know that plays are not always historically accurate, perhaps because the playwright depicts an incident which conflicts with what I had previously believed about the assassination of Julius Caesar. My suspension of belief has grounds, then, but that does not stop it from being voluntary. My decisions normally have grounds. 'Voluntary' is not a synonym for 'arbitrary'.

We can blame someone for not knowing something or for not having perceived something: 'You ought to know that', 'you ought to have seen that'. This is certainly equivalent to 'If you had looked carefully, or if you had reflected for a moment, you would have known that'. In a parallel way, one might be blamed for believing as a result of inadequate inquiry —'You wouldn't have believed that, if you had looked into the matter more closely.' One can be blamed, too, for claiming to know when one does not know, claiming to have perceived when one has not looked, claiming to have good grounds for a belief when one has no such grounds. But one cannot be blamed for knowing *prior* to comparing or for perceiving without looking; this is impossible. One can in contrast be blamed for believing before investigating—and it is then for *believing*, not merely for not investigating, that one is blamed.

So the attempt to assimilate the voluntariness of belief to the voluntariness of knowledge breaks down. It is not just that we can decide not to inquire; we can decide, it would seem, not to believe until we have inquired. Locke's dictum 'What upon full Examination I find the most probable, I cannot deny my Assent to' now assumes a fresh significance. What is the phrase 'upon full examination' doing in this dictum? If the analogy with perception and knowledge were a perfect one, then Locke should simply have written: 'What I find the most probable, I cannot deny my Assent to'. Instead, he adds the phrase 'after full examination' with the suggestion that I *can* deny my assent to what looks to be probable after a *less than full* examination. The parallel at this point is not, indeed, between Locke's theory of belief and his theory of knowledge but between his theory of belief and his theory of desire.

Our will, he suggested in the first edition of the *Essay*, is determined by what we immediately perceive to be the greater good; that is parallel to saying that our belief is determined by what we immediately perceive to be the greater probability. If we sometimes choose wrongly, Locke went on to add, this is because we do not always fully investigate the remote consequences of our actions. That is parallel to saying that if we sometimes believe wrongly this is because we do not always fully explore the probability of what we believe. As Locke's theory of the will stands in the first edition, however, 'choose wrongly' cannot mean 'choose in a manner in which the agent morally should not have chosen'. An outside observer may be in a position to remark: 'had he considered remoter consequences he would have chosen differently'. From the outsider's point of view the choice is then a wrong one. But the agent himself, and of necessity, has chosen what seemed to him the greater good; he cannot be blamed for doing so. It would have been *better* had he chosen otherwise. So in the Utopian sense of 'ought', he ought to have chosen differently. But in the moral sense of 'ought', no such judgement can be passed upon him. For how can the mind wait to explore before choosing, if it is always automatically determined by the greater good as it perceives it?

In the second edition of the *Essay*, Locke therefore introduced a fundamental change into his discussion of voluntary action. The mind, he now says, has a power to suspend its desires. '[D]uring this *suspension* of any desire', he writes, 'before the *will* be determined to action, and the action (which follows that determination) done, we have opportunity to examine, view, and judge of the good or evil of what we are going to do; and when, upon due *Examination*, we have judg'd we have done our duty . . . ; and 'tis not a fault, but a perfection of our nature to desire, will, and act according to the last result of a fair *Examination*' (II. XXI. 47).

We are no longer allowed to excuse ourselves, then, by explaining that we responded to what we perceived to be the greater good, that the remoter consequences we did not perceive. For we could have inhibited our impulse to act until we had explored further; the mere perception of a course of action as being to our greater good does not immediately and irresistably compel us to choose it.

The parallel between Locke on desire and Locke on belief should by now be obvious. From the point of view of an outside observer an agent believes wrongly if he believes as he would not have believed had he explored further. But the agent might reply: 'I believed as I had to believe on the evidence before me. If I had had your information, my belief would have been different. But it was not in fact before me. My belief may be *incorrect*, wrong in that sense, but none the less it was not wrong of me to hold it.' Locke's counter-argument, or so I am suggesting, would run something like this:

'During the suspension of any belief, we have an opportunity to examine, view and judge the probability of what we are being asked to believe; and when, upon due examination, we have judged, we have done our duty . . . ; it is not a fault but a perfection of our nature, to believe according to the last result of a fair examination.'

Our duty, then, is to hold ourselves back from choosing, or from believing, until we have considered the situation fully; people who do not do this can properly be blamed. But after such an examination, we cannot but choose what then seems to us the greater good, cannot but believe what seems to us most probable. And this is not as a result of some defect, some limitation on our freedom. On the contrary, it is 'a perfection of our nature' thus to believe. At this level, the truth of freedom is necessity.

One might argue, of course, that Locke was mistaken in supposing that we can voluntarily suspend our beliefs. Perhaps the true situation, as Professor Curley has suggested, is this: the arguments *pro* and *contra* are sometimes so balanced that our belief is suspended, as a balance is suspended by equal weights on either side.[1] So suspension of belief is no more voluntary than is believing or disbelieving, it is equally determined by the perceived probabilities.

But Locke cannot take this way out. We ought, on his view, to suspend our beliefs whenever we discover that they rest on unexamined grounds. This does not at all imply that the case against them is as strong as the case for them. That we do not yet know. The analogy is with suspending a policeman from his duties, pending inquiries. We have some ground for suspicion: that is all. Unless it is possible for human beings to suspend their belief in this sense, it is quite pointless to tell them that they ought not to accept beliefs on inadequate evidence. They will automatically believe whatever at that moment seems to them probable, with no choice in the matter. To those who reply that it is indeed pointless thus to rebuke them, that we *cannot* suspend our beliefs, Locke would have replied, I think, as he does to those who doubt whether we can suspend our desires: experience shows us that we can (II. XXI. 47).

Such an appeal to introspection might dissatisfy us; we may suspect Locke, both in relation to belief and desire, of employing, in the concept of suspension, an *ad hoc* device for reconciling his moral conviction that we ought to hold certain beliefs, make certain choices, with his theoretical conviction that our belief is always determined by our perception of probabilities, our choice by our perception of the greater good. But to describe him as proceeding in an *ad hoc* manner would be unfair;

[1] E. M. Curley in an essay on 'Descartes, Spinoza and the Ethics of Belief' in E. Freeman and M. Mandelbaum (eds.), *Spinoza: Essays in Interpretation* (La Salle, Illinois, 1975), p. 175.

that we can suspend our belief is certainly a common presumption. It might turn out to be mistaken, but it is certainly not the merely factitious product of a theoretician's dilemma. So, for example, in his *The Scientific Imagination*, Gerald Holton has argued that the scientist must learn both to suspend his belief and to suspend his disbelief, neither believing as soon as a plausible hypothesis presents itself nor disbelieving as soon as some accepted view is apparently overthrown by new evidence.[1] He does not take this view as a way out of problems in the theory of belief, but rather as a result of reflection on what actually happens within the institutions of science.

Locke would not be satisfied with the suggestion, made explicit by Bernard Williams, that we wrongly suppose ourselves to have some degree of control over our believing only because belief naturally passes over into public assertion and we do have a degree of control over what we publicly assert. As Locke emphasizes, there are many societies in which people cannot, without making a martyr of themselves, publicly assert their beliefs; they learn to be careful about what they say. If we live in such a society, it is still our duty, as Locke sees the situation, not to *believe* without examination. And in so far as to ascribe such a duty is to assume that belief can be voluntarily suspended, Locke is committed to the conclusion that belief lies under our control.

But our story is still not complete. Locke is more than a little perturbed by the fact that people's beliefs are so often not in accordance with the real probabilities, even if we take this to mean the probabilities as they would be estimated by someone who had scrupulously examined the available information, as distinct from the probabilities as an ideal human observer would estimate them. '[I]f', he writes, 'Assent be grounded on Likelihood, if the proper Object and Motive of our Assent be Probability [notice the transition from "grounded on" to "*proper* Object"] . . . it will be demanded, how Men come to give their Assents contrary to Probability' (XX. 1). Locke is convinced that he can satisfactorily reply to this objection. He attempts to do so, indeed, *before* he formulates his final view that belief is voluntary only in the sense in which knowledge is voluntary.

There are two distinct sets of cases to be considered, the first in which men do not have the relevant information before them, the second in which they have the relevant information before them but use, Locke says, 'wrong measures of probability'.

---

[1] Gerald Holton, *The Scientific Imagination* (Cambridge, 1978), p. 71.

In the first set of cases, Locke sees no theoretical difficulty. If people are so exhausted by hard labour or so politically restricted or so lacking in intelligence or so lazy that they are unable or unwilling to inquire, then it is only to be expected that the opinions they hold will be at variance with the real probabilities. For theological reasons, Locke has to maintain that these obstacles are never so formidable as to render a person incapable of discovering the fundamental truths of religion. But he can freely grant that such intellectually handicapped persons may, in respect to a wide range of their beliefs, hold beliefs which further inquiry would show them to be highly improbable—and, except where they are lazy, cannot be blamed for so believing.

The second class of cases Locke finds much more troublesome. There are men, he has to confess, who, 'even where the real Probabilities appear, and are plainly laid before them, do not admit of the conviction, nor yield unto manifest Reasons, but do either *epechein*, suspend their Assent, or give it to the less probable Opinion' (XX. 7). How can this be so if belief is an automatic response to the greater probability? Where such men go wrong, Locke tries to persuade us, is in *their estimates of probability*. They do not 'yield unto manifest reasons' because they assign probabilities wrongly. Note once again the close connection with Locke's theory of the will. He himself brings out the parallel. '[T]he Foundation of Errour', he writes, 'will lie in wrong Measures of Probability; as the Foundation of Vice in wrong Measures of Good' (XX. 16).

But how, in turn, does *this* mistake arise, this false belief that *p* has a greater probability than it really has? First, according to Locke, human beings tend to give too great a weight to general principles, principles which were instilled into them when they were children and which they therefore wrongly take to be innate and unquestionable. Indeed, they 'will disbelieve their own Eyes, renounce the Evidence of their Senses, and give their own Experience the lye, rather than admit of anything disagreeing with these sacred Tenets' (XX. 10). Locke roundly condemns those who act thus; at this point his theory of belief links with his rejection of innate principles. But this is not because they have *deliberately decided* to give a higher probability to these principles than they ought to give them; the principles were not deliberately adopted but were 'riveted there by long Custom and Education' (XX. 9). When Locke condemns such dogmatists—although with a measure of tolerance—it is in his usual fashion for *not inquiring*, not testing, not examining, their fundamental beliefs. This, he thinks, they could have done, had they so chosen.

Now, it is relatively easy to understand how a person educated all his life to hold a certain belief should ascribe to it so high a probability that nothing can outweigh it. But Locke includes the 'enthusiast' in this same category. 'Let an Enthusiast be principled, that he or his Teacher is inspired, and acted upon by an immediate Communication of the Divine Spirit, and you in vain bring the evidence of clear Reasons against his Doctrines' (XX. 10). In this instance, a person has *come to* assign a high probability to a quite preposterous proposition, a proposition which, furthermore, may be quite at variance with those principles to which, from childhood, he had been accustomed to assign a high probability. We cannot explain how *he* comes to make his mistakes by assimilating him to the person who was brought up to hold a particular belief.

Perhaps Locke has his classifications wrong. Perhaps he should have brought the enthusiast within the ambit of a third case he has described, when the objective grounds of probability do not accord with men's passions and appetites. 'Tell a Man, passionately in Love, that he is jilted; bring a score of Witnesses of the Falsehood of his Mistress, 'tis ten to one but three kind Words of hers shall invalidate all the Testimonies. *Quod volumus, facilè credimus; what suits our Wishes, is forwardly believed*' (XX. 12).

This, however, is more than a little startling. For we had been encouraged to assimilate belief to knowledge and to perception where, on Locke's view, passion has no such power. In the present instance, men do not deny the probabilities; at the same time they refuse to accept the conclusions which follow from them. Is this not a clear case of choosing to believe the less probable? The lover's friends would certainly describe the situation in these terms: 'he chose to believe his mistress rather than us'.

Locke tries to offer an alternative analysis of the situation, consistent with the general course of his argument as we have so far presented it: 'Not but that it is the Nature of the Understanding constantly to close with the more probable side, but yet a Man hath a Power to suspend and restrain its Enquiries, and not permit a full and satisfactory Examination, as far as the matter in Question is capable, and will bear it to be made.' But in the present instance this now-familiar tactic will not work. The evidence is *already* before the lover; he needs no more evidence. Neither does he suspend his belief: he believes his mistress and does not believe the witnesses, witnesses in whom, on other matters, he would have implicit faith.

So Locke tries a different tack, still working with his intellectualist conception of belief. In such cases, Locke argues, the person who faces the evidence squarely and yet says 'Although I cannot answer, I shall not yield', is still relying on grounds which seem to him probable. Fresh evidence, he will tell himself and his critics, may emerge, a hidden fallacy may be revealed, a witness may turn out to be unreliable, a conspiracy to be afoot. Locke is not suggesting that this is *always* a possible rejoinder. '[S]ome Proofs in Matter of Reason, being suppositions upon universal Experience, are so cogent and clear; and some Testimonies in Matter of Fact so universal, that [a man] cannot refuse his Assent' (XX. 15). But few philosophers, at least in their cooler moments, have ever supposed that it is *always* possible to choose what to believe. The only question is whether this is *ever* possible. And now Locke makes the concession we began by quoting: 'in Propositions, where though the Proofs in view are of most Moment, yet there are sufficient grounds, to suspect that there is either Fallacy in Words, or certain Proofs, as considerable, to be produced on the contrary side, there Assent, Suspense, or Dissent are often voluntary Actions'. The arguments we have before us in such instances we admit to be extremely powerful, and yet, as we say, we 'refuse to believe' the conclusion which would follow from them, we 'do not choose to believe' that it is true.

The fact that in such situations we so unselfconsciously use such expressions as 'refuse to believe', 'choose to believe' does not, of course, finally settle the matter. These expressions might rest on intellectual confusions, myths about our own capacities; or they might be idiomatic ways of talking, misleading only if we (wrongly) take them literally. Perhaps Locke need not have made his concession. Very strong evidence has been produced, let us say, that a political leader we have been accustomed to admire has betrayed us. We say that we 'do not choose to believe' or 'prefer not to believe' that he is guilty. But all this may mean is that out of loyalty we are not prepared to *admit* that he is guilty.

Such an interpretation would link very neatly with the set of observations with which Locke ends this section of his *Essay*. After all his explanations, he is still worried about the fact that men have so many false beliefs, beliefs contrary to probabilities of which they are well aware, even although, in his view, their beliefs are naturally determined by the evidence before them. What men call their 'beliefs', he therefore suggests, are very often not beliefs at all but expressions of party loyalty. 'They are resolved to stick to a Party, that Education or Interest has engaged them in; and there, like the common Soldiers of an Army, shew their Courage and Warmth, as their Leaders direct, without ever examining, or so much as knowing the Cause they contend for' (XX. 18).

It is not just that such 'common soldiers' have acquiesced without reflection in some current opinion, like the man who acquiesces in the view that Richard III was a hunch-back. For he at least understands what he is acquiescing in; he gives the proposition enough attention to be confident that it is not utterly ridiculous, even if he does not closely examine its truth. In contrast, Locke is suggesting, the majority of the members of a party or a Church do not even *understand* the views to which their membership commits them. Their so-called 'beliefs' are, on their lips, mere catch-cries, expressing their resolution to stick by their party. So their apparent capacity to believe what cuts clean across the evidence is improperly so described. It is a capacity, only, to utter certain phrases when their party or Church calls upon them to do so. And if 'I believe p', can sometimes thus be equated with 'I stand by the party which asserts p', then equally 'I refuse to believe that p', 'I like to believe that p', 'you ought to believe that p', can be expressions of, or exhortations to, loyalty, whether to a person or a party.

Locke puts forward a very similar argument in his *Commonplace Book*.[1] He then asks us to consider the case of a man who adheres, without critical reflection, to what Locke calls 'a collection of certain professions'—let us say the Thirty-nine Articles or the Westminster Confession. Such an adherence, Locke tells us, 'is not in truth believing but a profession to believe'.

Yet, one naturally objects, if we ask the loyal adherent: 'Do you believe p?', he will certainly, and sincerely, reply 'Yes'. Furthermore, if the belief is of the kind that carries actions as a consequence, he will engage in those actions; he will not merely tell us that God is present in the consecrated wafer, to take Locke's own example of transubstantiation, he will approach communion reverently. If we ask him to explain to us in detail

[1] Lord King, *Life*, ii, pp. 76–7.

in what the doctrine of the Real Presence consists, he will no doubt rapidly become confused, should we not be satisfied with the stock-catechism answers. But does this imply that he does not actually believe in the Real Presence? One is reluctant either on the one side to identify a merely habitual response—in which utterances 'are made, actions performed, but without any understanding whatsoever'—with a genuine belief or on the other side to permit oneself to speak of 'beliefs' only in those instances where the situation has been fully comprehended. Some degree of understanding, some capacity to answer relevant questions, seems to be required for a genuine belief. But *what* degree of understanding is quite another matter. Unless we put the criteria high, we shall not find it possible to avoid the conclusion, which Locke wants to avoid, that a great many people hold quite absurd beliefs. Yet if we do set them high, we make it impossible for anybody to believe, as distinct from merely parroting phrases, unless he has considerable intellectual gifts, a conclusion which seems quite monstrous.

So far, I have had nothing to say about the chapter on 'Enthusiasm' which Locke introduced into the fourth edition of the *Essay* immediately prior to that chapter on 'Wrong Assent, or Errour' to which our attention has latterly been directed. One is indeed tempted to pass it over as of merely historical interest. But in fact it entirely disrupts the argument he has so far developed and continues to develop in the chapter which now succeeds it. In discussing the enthusiasts we might expect him to experience his greatest difficulties in defending his intellectualist account of belief. And this is precisely what we do find. We find, too, confirmation of our suggestion that the enthusiast should be classified with the lover who believes against the evidence. Locke now begins to describe rational belief not in terms of a purely intellectual weighing-up but rather in terms of the operations of a certain form of passion— the love of truth.

No doubt, he links his new emphasis on passion with the course of his previous argument. There is, he says, one unerring mark of the lover of truth: 'The not entertaining any Proposition with greater assurance than the Proofs it is built upon will warrant' (XIX. 1). But whereas we had once been given to understand that human beings were so constituted as inevitably thus to adjust their degree of assurance to the evidence, we are now told that 'there are very few lovers of Truth for Truths sake, even amongst those, who perswade themselves that they are so'. What happens, then, when men believe a proposition with greater assurance than the evidence for it warrants? In such instances, Locke now informs us, '''tis plain all that surplusage of assurance is owing to some other Affection, and not to the Love of Truth'. Or again, 'Whatsoever Credit or Authority we give to any Proposition more than it receives from the Principles or Proofs it supports it self upon, is owing to our Inclinations that way, and is so far a Derogation from the Love of Truth as such.' That dictum which in earlier versions of the *Essay* was little more than a passing remark—'what suits our wishes is forwardly believed'—comes to occupy the centre of the stage. It is no longer surprising that believing, as Locke's argument proceeded, came to be parallel to desiring rather than to knowing. In rational men, men inspired by the love of truth, belief is no doubt founded on the evidence and nothing but the evidence. If belief is in their case ever voluntary, it is only so in those very special instances in which they continue to believe, with the probabilities against them, in the expectation that fresh information will turn up. But such lovers of truth, Locke now thinks, are rare. What he is now prepared explicitly to call 'groundless fancies' play a much greater part in human life than he had at first been prepared to admit. Indeed, whereas a belief had at first been *defined* as a proposition received as true *upon arguments and proofs*, this definition, it would now appear, applies only to rational, or relatively rational, beliefs; men can believe from inclination, or at the very least they can believe from inclination with much greater assurance than they should believe. (And in the case of the enthusiast, with his 'groundless fancies', the degree of assurance should be zero.)

Can they be blamed for believing? Locke seems to take it for granted that our inclinations lie in some measure under our control. 'He that would seriously set upon the search of Truth', he writes, 'ought in the first Place to prepare his Mind with a Love of it' (XIX. 1)—as if this 'preparation of the mind', with the subduing of inclinations which it entails, lies within our power. 'He that hath not a mastery over his inclinations', he tells us in *Some Thoughts Concerning Education*, ' . . . for the sake of what reason tells him is fit to be done, wants the true principle of virtue and industry'.[1]

Finally, a word or two about 'faith', in the narrow sense of the word, the acceptance of a belief because it is taken to be

[1] *Some thoughts Concerning Education*, § 45, ed. F. W. Cornforth (London, 1964), p. 64.

divinely revealed. Historically speaking, this has occupied the very centre of the debate about whether men can decide to believe. Many Christian theologians, from Clement of Alexandria to Newman, have thought it a central assumption of Christianity that assent lies in a man's power, that men can choose to believe what God teaches them, even when it is contrary to experience, perhaps even to reason. For they have wanted to blame 'men of little faith', the Doubting Thomases of this world.[1] And they were conscious of what Jesus is reported as saying in Mark: that men are to be saved for believing, damned for not believing (16: 15–16). How could this be, if men are not free to believe? Not all theologians, of course, have taken this view. Faith, many of them have argued, is a grace of God; men can believe only when God enables, or perhaps compels, them to do so. If Jesus condemned them for not believing, this is only to express God's mysterious judgement upon them. Or like Aquinas they have sought to compromise. Faith he describes as 'an act of the intellect assenting to Divine truth at the command of the will moved by the grace of God',[2] an act of free choice, even although a choice men can make only when God permits them to do so. But when philosophers and theologians have asserted man's freedom to believe, this has most often been in order to leave room, as Locke also wants to do, for condemning infidelity. Or else, as in Clifford's case, for condemning credulity as the wrongful making of a decision.

Locke, however, and without calling on divine grace, does not make of faith an exception to his view that the rational man will believe only with a degree of assurance proportional to the evidence. Once again he begins from the case of knowledge. '[N]o Proposition', he says, 'can be received for Divine Revelation, or obtain the Assent due to all such, if it be contradictory to our clear intuitive Knowledge' (XVIII. 5). It is only reason that can tell us a particular book is divinely inspired; and no evidence that it is so inspired can be as clear and certain as the principles of reason itself. 'Nothing that is contrary to, and inconsistent with the

[1] That assent, or belief, is an act of the will has continued to be a very widely held doctrine amongst Roman Catholic philosophers. So Lonergan tells us that 'it is a free and responsible decision of the will to believe a given proposition as probably or certainly true or false', B. J. F. Lonergan: *Insight* (2nd edn. rev. London, 1958), p. 709. The extent of conflict on this point is brought out in Rodney Needham, *Belief, Language, and Experience* (Oxford, 1972), pp. 81–6.

[2] *Summa Theologica*: 'Of the Act of Faith', Second Part of the Second Part, Question 2, Article 9, Dominican translation.

clear and self-evident Dictates of Reason, has a Right to be urged, or assented to, as a Matter of Faith' (XVIII. 10). We are to have faith in what revelation tells us, only if all we can set against it are '*probable Conjectures*' (XVIII. 8).

Here, very obviously, Locke is writing in moralistic terms. 'Nothing that is contrary to the Dictates of Reason has a *right* to be assented to.' It is not at all being suggested that we *cannot* believe what is contrary to reason. '*I believe, because it is impossible*, might', he says, 'pass for a Sally of Zeal', but it 'would prove a very ill Rule for Men to chuse their Opinions, or Religion by' (XVIII. 11). A 'very ill rule' no doubt, but on the view from which he originally set out, it would be not only 'ill' but *impossible* to adopt such a rule. In short, the existence of the enthusiast constantly undermines Locke's hopeful view of man, as a being who naturally, and inevitably, responds to the most probable hypothesis—much as the very existence of twentieth-century enthusiasts has undermined the similar confidence we partly inherited from Locke himself, but without paying adequate attention to his vacillations and reservations.

There can be no doubt, I think, that Locke would have liked consistently to maintain two theses, the first that rational human beings will regulate their degree of assurance in a proposition so that it accords with the evidence—the ideal of an objective science, the Enlightenment ideal. The second, that human beings are so constituted as naturally to do this, were created rational, that they go wrong only when some of the evidence is not before them. But he finds it impossible to reconcile this second thesis with his experience of the actual irrationality of human beings, brought home to him with peculiar sharpness by the Civil War and, more particularly, by the 'enthusiasm' of the Puritan sectaries. At first, he does what he can to reconcile his theories with his experience by suggesting that what, from the point of view of better-informed observers, are irrational beliefs have a rational foundation, that they rest upon errors of fact rather than errors of judgement—errors of fact arising either out of ignorance or the assignment of wrong measures of probability. If only men could bring themselves to inquire, he argues in this spirit, they would cease to hold irrational beliefs. But then he still has on his hands a residue of cases, in which men have all the evidence before them which they could possibly need, and yet still believe irrationally. Perhaps, he is at one point led to suggest, they do not under these circumstances *believe*, in the proper sense, at all; they merely mouth phrases.

But it is very hard to take this view about an ardent enthusiast, convinced that he is personally inspired by God. And so in the end Locke is led to conclude that men can believe falsely, not as the result of having inadequate evidence, but as a result of being dominated by powerful inclinations. And so he is gradually driven into a new picture of belief, in which it is no longer a weaker form of knowledge, but rather, like desire in Locke's second-edition account of desire, an attempt to remove uneasiness, to satisfy our inclinations. The rational man is then the man who is dominated by a passion for truth, as distinct from party passions. Conscious of the fact that his beliefs are often based upon evidence which from the point of view of an ideal observer is inadequate, such a rational man will be tolerant, as the enthusiast, confusing his beliefs with knowledge, will not be tolerant. But at the same time the rational man will *blame* the enthusiast, whether on Locke's first view, for not properly inquiring or, on Locke's second view, for not properly controlling his inclination to believe beyond the evidence.

LEIBNIZ AND DESCARTES: PROOF AND ETERNAL TRUTHS

By IAN HACKING

LEIBNIZ knew what a proof is. Descartes did not. Due attention to this fact helps resolve some elusive problems of interpretation. That is not my chief aim today. I am more interested in prehistory than history. Leibniz's concept of proof is almost the same as ours. It did not exist until about his time. How did it become possible? Descartes, according to Leibniz, furnished most of the technology required for the formation of this concept, yet deliberately shied away from anything like our concept of proof. I contend that Descartes, in his implicit rejection of our idea of proof, and Leibniz, in his excessive attachment to it, are both trying to meet a fundamental malaise in seventeenth-century epistemology. I speak of a malaise rather than a problem or difficulty, for it was not formulated and was perhaps not formulable. But although these unformulated preconditions for the concept of proof are forgotten and even arcane, many facts of the resulting theories of proof are familiar enough. Leibniz was sure that mathematical truth is constituted by proof while Descartes thought that truth conditions have nothing to do with demonstration. We recognize these competing doctrines in much modern philosophy of mathematics. The way in which the two historical figures enacted many of our more recent concerns has not gone unnoticed: Yvon Belaval deliberately begins his important book on Leibniz and Descartes with a long chapter called 'Intuitionisme et formalisme'.[1] There are plenty more parallels there for the drawing. I find this no coincidence, for I am afflicted by a conjecture, both unsubstantiated and unoriginal, that the 'space' of a philosophical problem is largely fixed by the conditions that made it possible. A problem is individuated only by using certain concepts, and the preconditions for the emergence of those concepts are almost embarrassingly determining of what can be done with them. Solutions, countersolutions, and dissolutions are worked out in a space

[1] *Leibniz critique de Descartes*, Paris, 1960.

whose properties are not recognized but whose dimensions are as secure as they are unknown. I realize that there is no good evidence for the existence of conceptual 'space' nor of 'preconditions' for central concepts. Nothing in what follows depends on succumbing to the conjecture that there are such things. The Dawes Hicks lecture is dedicated to history and I shall do history, but I do want to warn that my motive for doing so is the philosophy of mathematics and its prehistory.

In saying that Leibniz knew what a proof is, I mean that he anticipated in some detail the conception of proof that has become dominant in our century. He is commonly said to have founded symbolic logic. He occupies the first forty entries in Alonzo Church's definitive *Bibliography of Symbolic Logic*. I do not have that logical activity in mind. Most seventeenth-century wrestling with quantifiers, relations, combinatorics, and the syllogism seems clumsy or even unintelligible to the most sympathetic modern reader. In contrast Leibniz's ideas about proof sound just right.

A proof, thought Leibniz, is valid in virtue of its form, not its content. It is a sequence of sentences beginning with identities and proceeding by a finite number of steps of logic and rules of definitional substitution to the theorem proved.[1] He experimented with various rules of logic and sometimes changed his mind on which 'first truths' are admissible. He was not able to foresee the structure of the first order predicate logic. He unwittingly made one of our more beautiful theorems—the completeness of predicate logic—into a definition through his equivalence between provability and truth in all possible worlds. My claim for Leibniz is only that he knew what a proof was. He was not even good at writing down proofs that are formally correct, for by nature he was hasty, in contrast to Descartes who despised formalism and who is nearly always formally correct.

The Leibnizian understanding of proof did not much exist before his time. Yet so well did Leibniz understand proof that he could offer metamathematical demonstrations of consistency using the fact that a contradiction cannot be derived in any

[1] This frequently occurring theme is expressed, for example, in the letter to Conring of 19 Mar. 1678, *P.* I, 194. See also *P.* VII, 194 and *O.* 518. On the importance of form rather than content, see the letters to Tshirnhaus, e.g. May 1678, *M.* IV, 451. (*P.* = *Die Philosophischen Schriften von G. W. Leibniz*, ed. G. Gerhardt. *O.* = *Opuscules et fragments inédits de Leibniz*, ed. L. Couturat. *M.* = *Mathematische Schriften*, ed. G. Gerhardt.)

number of steps from premisses of a given form.[1] He understood that a proof of a necessary proposition must be finite, and made an important part of his philosophy hinge on the difference between finite and infinite proofs. We owe to him the importance of the definition of necessity as reduction to contradiction, and the corresponding definition of possibility as freedom from contradiction, understood as the inability to prove a contradiction in finitely many steps. Proof is not only finite but computable, and the checking of proofs is called a kind of arithmetic. Leibniz even saw the importance of representing ideas and propositions by a recursive numbering scheme.[2] His invention of topology is motivated by a theory of the notation needed for valid proof.[3] He is not alone in any of these observations but he did have the gift of synthesizing and stating some of their interconnections. In asking how these ideas became possible it is immaterial whether they are the ideas of a single man. It suffices that they are novel and become widespread in the era of Leibniz, but it is convenient to have an Olympian figure who so perfectly epitomizes this new understanding.

Leibniz himself has a plausible explanation of why the concept of proof emerged at this time. Insight into the nature of proof is not to be expected when geometry is the standard of rigour. Geometrical demonstrations can appear to rely on their content. Their validity may seem to depend on facts about the very shapes under study, and whose actual construction is the aim of the traditional Euclidean theorems. A Cartesian breakthrough changed this. Descartes algebrized geometry. Algebra is specifically a matter of getting rid of some content. Hence in virtue of Descartes' discovery, geometrical proof can be conceived as purely formal. Leibniz thought that Descartes had stopped short, and did not see his way through to a completely general abstract Universal Characteristic in which proofs could be conducted,

and which renders truth stable, visible and irresistible, so to speak, as on a mechanical basis ... Algebra, which we rightly hold in such esteem, is only a part of this general device. Yet algebra accomplished this much —that we cannot err even if we wish and that truth can be grasped as if pictured on paper with the aid of a machine. I have come to understand that everything of this kind which algebra proves is due only

[1] For example in notes written in Nov. 1676, intended for discussion with Spinoza. *P.* VII, 261.
[2] *Lingua Generalis*, Feb. 1678, *O.* 277. Cf. L. Couturat, *La Logique de Leibniz*, Paris, 1901, ch. III.   [3] To Huygens, 8 Sept. 1679, *M.* II, 17; cf. *P.* V, 178.

to a higher science, which I now usually call a *combinatorial characteristic*.[1]

'Nothing more effective,' Leibniz ventures to say, 'can well be conceived for the perfection of the human mind.' Insight becomes irrelevant to recognizing the validity of a proof, and truth has become 'mechanical'. Two trains of thought parallel this conception of proof. One has long been known: Leibniz's belief that there exists a proof, possibly infinite, for every truth. Sometimes readers have inferred that the Universal Characteristic was intended to settle every question whereas in fact Leibniz continues the letter quoted above saying that after the Characteristic is complete, 'men will return to the investigation of nature alone, which will never be completed'. The second train of thought concerns probability. Leibniz did often say that when the Characteristic is available disputes would be resolved by calculation. Sometimes these calculations would be *a priori* demonstrations but more usually they would work out the probability of various opinions relative to the available data. In surprisingly many details Leibniz's programme resembles the work of Rudolf Carnap on inductive logic.[2] I shall argue at the end of this lecture that the Leibnizian conceptions of proof and probability have intimately related origins. For the present I shall restrict discussion to proof.

Although the conception of proof and probability is partly familiar, there is a point at which most admirers of Leibniz stop:

> Every true proposition that is not identical or true in itself can be proved *a priori* with the help of axioms or propositions that are true in themselves and with the help of definitions or ideas.[3]

'Every' here includes all contingent truths. Moreover, Leibniz thought one does not fully understand a truth until one knows the *a priori* proofs. Since the 'analysis of concepts' required for proof of contingent propositions is 'not within our power', we cannot fully understand contingent truths. In these passages Leibniz is not giving vent to some sceptic's claim that only what is proven is reliable. Leibniz is no sceptic. He is not even an epistemologist. You need a proof to understand something because a proof actually constitutes the analysis of concepts which in turn determines the truth, 'or I know not what truth

---

[1] To Oldenburg, 28 Dec. 1675, *M*. I, 84.

[2] For references see my 'The Leibniz-Carnap program for inductive logic', *Jl. Phil.* lxviii, 1971, 597.

[3] *P*. VII, 300.

is'.[1] Moreover a proof gives the reason why something is true, and indeed the cause of the truth. Truth, reason, cause, understanding, analysis, and proof are inextricably connected. It is part of my task to trace the origin of these connections. The connections are not automatic then or now. To illustrate this we need only take the contrasting doctrines of Descartes.

Leibniz thought that truth is constituted by proof. Descartes thought proof irrelevant to truth. This comes out nicely at the metaphorical level. Leibniz's God, in knowing a truth, knows the infinite analysis and thereby knows the proof. That is what true knowledge is. Leibniz's God recognizes proofs. Descartes' God is no prover. A proof might help a person see some truth, but only because people have poor intellectual vision. It used to be held that angels did not need to reason. Although commendably reticent about angels, Descartes has just such an attitude to reasoning. He is at one with the mathematician G. H. Hardy,

Proofs are what Littlewood and I call gas, rhetorical flourishes designed to affect psychology . . . devices to stimulate the imagination of pupils.[2]

Naturally Descartes says little about demonstration. Much of what he says is consistent with the doctrines advanced in the *Regulae*. Intuition and deduction are distinguished. Elementary truths of arithmetic can be intuited by almost anyone. Consequences may also be intuited. Deduction requires the intuition of initial propositions and consequential steps. The modern reader tends to equate intuition and deduction with axiom and theorem proved, but this is to see matters in a Leibnizian mould. The Cartesian distinction is chiefly psychological. One man might require deduction where another would intuit. In either case the end product is perception of truth. Some Cartesian scholars have recently debated whether the *cogito ergo sum* is inference or intuition or something else again.[3] Descartes does give varying accounts of this famous *ergo* but it is completely immaterial to him whether one man needs to infer where another intuits directly. The point of the *cogito*, as the *Discourse*

---

[1] To Arnauld, 14 July(?), 1686, *P.* II, 56.

[2] 'Mathematical Proof', *Mind*, xxviii, 1928, 18.

[3] For example, H. G. Frankfurt, 'Descartes' discussion of his existence in the second meditation', *Phil. Rev.* 1966, 333. A. Kenny, *Descartes*, New York, ch. 3. Jaako Hintikka, '*Cogito ergo sum*, inference or performance?' *Phil. Rev.* lxxi, 1962, 3–32. I agree with André Gombay, from whom I have much profited in conversation about Descartes. '*Cogito ergo sum*, inference or argument?' in *Cartesian Studies*, ed. R. J. Butler, Oxford, 1972.

informs us, is to display a truth one cannot doubt. Then one may inquire what, in this truth, liberates us from doubt. The intuition/inference/performative controversy is misguided because Descartes is indifferent to what sort of 'gas' induces clear and distinct perception. However you get there, when you see with clarity and distinctness you note that there is no other standard of truth than the natural light of reason. Leibniz, although granting some sense to 'what is called the natural light of reason',[1] inevitably observed that Descartes 'did not know the genuine source of truths nor the general analysis of concepts'.[2]

The Cartesian independence of truth from proof is illustrated by Descartes' unorthodox view on the eternal truths. These comprise the truths of arithmetic, algebra, and geometry, and usually extend to the laws of astronomy, mechanics, and optics. Contemporary authorities like Suarez taught that eternal truths are independent of the will of God. All the eternal verities are hypothetical. If there are any triangles, their interior angles must sum to two right angles. Since God is free to create or not to create triangles, this hypothetical necessity is no constraint on his power.[3] Descartes, although cautious in expressing opinions at odds with received doctrine, disagreed. The eternal truths depend upon the will of God, and God could have made squares with more or fewer than four sides. As we might express it, the eternal truths are necessary, but they are only contingently necessary.

Even if God has willed that some truths should be necessary, this does not mean that he willed them necessarily, for it is one thing to will that they be necessary, and quite another to will them necessarily.[4]

I very much like the way that Emile Bréhier[5] uses this theory about eternal truth in order to explain away the Cartesian 'circle' alleged, in the first instance, by Arnauld. The circle goes like this: from the clarity and distinctness of the third meditation it follows that God exists, but clarity and distinctness can be counted on only if there is a good God. Many commentators interrupt this simple-minded circle by saying that God's veracity

[1] To Sophia Charlotte, 1702, *P.* VI, 501.

[2] To Philip, Dec. 1679, *P.* IV. 282.

[3] F. Suarez, *Disputationes Metaphysicae*, 1597. Cf. T. J. Cronin, *Objective Being in Descartes and in Suarez*, Analecta Gregoriana 154, Rome, 1966.

[4] To Mesland, 2 May 1644. Other texts on eternal truths are as follows. To Mersenne, 6 May and 27 May 1630 and 27 May 1638. Reply to *Objections* V and VI. *Principles* xlviii–xlix.

[5] 'La creation des verités éternelles', *Rev. Phil.* cxxiii, 1937, 15.

is not needed when we are actually perceiving truth with clarity and distinctness. God comes in only when we turn our minds to another thought. This leaves open the question of the role that God plays when we are thus distracted. There are several competing interpretations. André Gombay uses this comparison.[1] In moments of passionate love a man (such as the husband in Strindberg's play, *The Father*) cannot doubt that his wife is faithful. But at more humdrum moments he doubts her love. What is his doubt? (*a*) His memory is playing tricks; the feeling of passionate certainty never occurred. (*b*) He remembers correctly his passionate conviction, but subsequently feels that he was misled by his passion. No matter how convinced he was then, he was wrongly convinced. (*c*) She was true to him at that passionate moment, but is no longer so. In the case of Cartesian doubt, recent commentators correctly rule out doubts of kind (*a*): God is no guarantor of memory. Gombay, probably rightly, favours (*b*). But doubt of kind (*c*) is instructive. Bréhier proposes that God is needed to ensure that an 'eternal truth', once perceived clearly and distinctly, *stays* true.

No set of texts tells conclusively for or against the Bréhier reading. This in itself shows how far Descartes separates proof from truth. What would happen to the proof of *p* if *p*, previously proven, went false? We can imagine that in the evolution of the cosmos Euclid's fifth postulate was true, relative to some assigned metric, and subsequently ceased to be true. At least this remains, we think: if a complete set of Euclidean axioms is true, the Pythagorean theorem is true too. That necessary connection between axiom and theorem cannot itself be contingent. Descartes disagreed. God is at liberty to create a Euclidean non-Pythagorean universe. We owe to Leibniz the clear statement that if not-*p* entails a contradiction then *p* is necessary and indeed necessarily necessary. Descartes grants that it is unintelligible how *p* can entail contradiction and still be true. But this unintelligibility shows the weakness of our minds. Leibniz caustically dismisses this view of modality.[2] It betrays, he thought, a lack of comprehension of the very concepts of necessity, contradiction, and proof.

Not only did Descartes acknowledge no dependence of necessary truth on proof; he also challenged accepted modes of presenting proof. He favoured 'analysis' rather than 'synthesis'. His

---

[1] 'Counter privacy and the evil genius', read to the Moral Sciences Club, 30 May 1973.

[2] *Monadology*, § 46.

doctrine is sufficiently hard to understand that Gerd Buchdahl distinguishes radically different Cartesian meanings for 'analysis',[1] but even if Descartes ought to have distinguished meanings of the word, he intended to be unequivocal. Synthesis is deduction, whose paradigm is Euclid. Deduction may bully a reader into agreement, but it does not teach how the theorem was discovered. Only analysis can do that. Descartes subscribed to the standard myth that the Greeks had a secret art of discovery.[2] The new algebraic geometry rediscovered it. He called it analytic geometry, as we still do. Its method is to:

suppose the solution already effected, and give names to all the lines that seem needful for the construction . . . then, making no distinction between known and unknown lines, we must unravel the difficulty in any way that shows most naturally the relations between these lines, until we find it possible to express a quantity in two ways.[3]

Then we solve the equation. Analysis is a mode of discovery of unknowns, and the arguments of the *Geometry* show how solutions can be obtained. Descartes thought that the physicist postulating causes on the basis of observed effects may be doing analysis, and he maintained that the *Meditations* furnish another example of analysis.

The Cartesian notion of analysis underwent strange transformations. The fact that Euclidean synthesis was deemed to depend on content as well as form is well illustrated by Descartes' own observations that in geometry the primary notions of synthetic proofs 'harmonize with our senses'. The point of all those 'minute subdivisions of propositions' is not even to ensure that the proof is sound. It is to render citation easy 'and thus make people recollect earlier stages of the argument even against their will'.[4] Synthetic proofs work partly because we have sensible representations of what we are proving and are thus unfit for metaphysics which uses abstract concepts. Yet by a strange inversion, it is Cartesian analysis that enables Leibniz to argue that proof is entirely a matter of form, and to apply this thought to deductive proof in general, including synthesis. Moreover, what he calls the analysis of concepts proceeds by what Descartes would have called synthetic demonstration!

Descartes wanted good ways to find out the truth and was indifferent to the logical status of his methods. This is well

[1] *Metaphysics and the Philosophy of Science*, Oxford, 1969, ch. 3.
[2] At the end of the reply to the second set of *Objections*.
[3] From the beginning of the *Geometry*.
[4] Op. cit., n. 2.

illustrated by yet another kind of 'analysis'. Traditionally science was supposed to proceed by demonstration of effects from causes stated in first principles. In practice the more successful scientists were increasingly guessing at causes on the basis of effects according to what we can now call 'the hypothetico-deductive method'. When challenged Descartes said that this too is a kind of 'demonstration', at least according to 'common usage', as opposed to the 'special meaning that philosophers give' to the word 'demonstration'. In reality, says Descartes, there are two kinds of demonstration, one from causes to effects, in which we prove the effect from the cause, and the other from effect to cause, in which we explain the effect by postulating a cause.[1]

There was a pressing practical problem for the second kind of so-called demonstration. As his correspondent put it, 'nothing is easier than to fit a cause to an effect'. To which Descartes replied that 'there are many effects to which it is easy to fit separate causes, but it is not always so easy to fit a single cause to many effects'. This thought was worked up by Leibniz into the theory of 'architectonic' reasoning.[2] We seek those hypotheses that would be attractive to the Architect of the World, who has a mania for maximizing the variety of phenomena governed by laws of nature, while minimizing the complexity of those selfsame laws.

On such questions of method there does not seem, in perspective, very much at issue between the two philosophers. But they have radically different theories of what they are finding out. Leibniz supposes that truths are constituted by proof, and so proof is essentially linked to truth, while Descartes imagines that truths exist independently of any proof. However, we shall not find the origin of this difference in what might be called the philosophy of mathematics, but in what we should now call the philosophy of science. The very success of scientific activity in the early seventeenth century had created a crisis in man's understanding of what he knows. In the medieval formulations, adapted from Aristotle, knowledge or science was arrived at by demonstration from first principles. It demonstrated effects from causes, and its propositions were universal in form and were necessarily true. In giving the causes, it gave the reasons for belief, and also the reasons why the proposition proved is true. As well as arithmetic and geometry, science included

---

[1] To Morin, 13 July 1638.
[2] *Tentamentum Anagogicum*, 1696, *P.* VII, 270.

astronomy, mechanics, and optics. This did not mean that one was supposed to do all one's mechanics *a priori*, for it might need ample experience to grasp the first principles of the universe. Francis Bacon furnishes a good example of a thinker trying to preserve this old ontology, insisting that instead of being dogmatic, the scientist must survey large quantities of experiences before he ventures to guess at the axioms, common notions, and first principles. What one is aiming at, however, is a body of universal and necessary axioms which will, when recognized and understood, have the character of self-evidence.

Bacon's methodology is a despairing attempt to save the old theory of truth on its own ground. Increasingly men of science are not doing what they are supposed to be doing. Among what I shall call the high sciences, astronomy, mechanics, and optics, there is a dogmatic school maintaining the Aristotelian physics. It is shattered by new theories which do not merely contradict the old physics but do not even have the same kind of propositions that the old physics sought after. Moreover, among the low sciences, medicine and alchemy, whose practitioners are what Bacon scornfully called the empirics, there has developed a set of practices and concepts that are unintelligible on the old model of knowledge.

Descartes' curious assertions about 'false hypotheses' illustrate how far he has come from traditional views. He says at length in his *Principles*, and throughout his life to various correspondents, that the chief hypotheses of his physics are strictly false, and may be regarded as a kind of fable.[1] It is common to construe this as a safety net spread out after the Galilean scandal. Is it? Hypotheses serve as the basis for deducing true effects, but are not themselves to be asserted as true. Many ancient writers, including Archimedes, base their demonstrations on hypotheses that are strictly false or so Descartes says. Perhaps he is merely seeking bedfellows in support of political caution. I see no reason to think so. Leibniz says that if they worked Descartes' 'false hypotheses' would be like cryptograms for solving the regularity of phenomena,[2] and he also says that Descartes is just wrong in changing the direction of physics to a search for false hypotheses. In short the Cartesian view was taken literally by the next generation of readers.

If Descartes means what he says everything has been turned upside down. Science was to make the world and its truths

---

[1] *Principles*, xliii–xlvii, and, e.g., To Mesland, May 1645.
[2] To Conring, 19 Mar. 1678, *P.* I, 194.

intelligible. From universal first principles concerning essence and cause and the true being of things one was to deduce the effects and their reasons, making intelligible the variety of general phenomena present to us. The first principles were to get at the very core of truth. But now the core evaporates, turns into a mere sham, a cryptogram of falsehoods. New merits have to be found for science, chief among them, in the seventeenth century, being the virtue of predictive power. In the traditional theory of truth, predictive power did not matter much because science was demonstrating necessities. When it abandons its ability to give reasons and causes by way of first principles, all it can do is provide us with predictions.

The evaporation of truth is what I have called the malaise or even the crisis in the early seventeenth century. We have been accustomed, especially in Britain, to notice the epistemological worries of the period. In fact men wrote treatises not of epistemology but of methodology. The methodology was an attempt to tell how to do what was in fact being done, and how to do it better. The Cartesian titles such as *Rules for direction of the mind*, or *Discourse on Method*, are characteristic of the time. Underneath these works runs not the problem of British empiricism-scepticism, 'How can I ever know?' It is rather, 'What is knowledge, what is truth, are there such things?'

Reconsider the situation of Descartes. We have usually read him as an ego, trapped in the world of ideas, trying to find out what corresponds to his ideas, and pondering questions of the form, 'How can I ever know?' Underneath his work lies a much deeper worry. Is there any truth at all, even in the domain of ideas? The eternal truths, he tells us, are 'perceptions . . . that have no existence outside of our thought'.[1] But in our thought they are, in a sense, isolated perceptions. They may be systematized by synthesis but this has nothing to do with their truth. The body of eternal truths which encompassed mathematics, neo-Aristotelian physics and perhaps all reality was a closely knit self-authenticating system of truth, linked by demonstration. For Descartes there are only perceptions which are ontologically unrelated to anything and moreover are not even candidates for having some truth outside my mind. One is led, I think, to a new kind of worry. I cannot doubt an eternal truth when I am contemplating it clearly and distinctly. But when I cease to contemplate, it is a question whether there is truth *or* falsehood in what I remember having perceived. Bréhier

---

[1] *Principles*, I. xlviii.

suggested that demonstrated propositions may go false. It seems
to me that Cartesian propositions, rendered lone and isolated, are
in an even worse state. Perhaps neither they nor their negations
have any truth at all. They exist in the mind only as perceptions.
Do they have any status at all when not perceived? When
demonstration cannot unify and give 'substance' to these truths,
the constancy of a veracious God who wills this truth suddenly
assumes immense importance. We have long been familiar with
the role of God as the willing agent that causes Berkeley's perceptions. We know Leibniz required the mind of God as the
arena in which the essences of possible worlds compete for
existence, saying indeed that

neither the essences nor the so-called eternal truths about them are
fictitious but exist in a certain region of ideas, if I may so call it, namely
in God himself.[1]

I am suggesting that Descartes' veracious God is needed not
just to guarantee our beliefs, but also to ensure that there is
some truth to believe. I do not claim this as a worked out
Cartesian thought but rather as an underlying response to
the breakdown in the traditional conception of knowledge.

Descartes was almost ingenuously radical. Faced by the fact
that the new science was not Aristotelian knowledge or *scientia*,
he abolished the traditional concepts even where they did work,
namely in arithmetic and geometry. Leibniz, in contrast, was
ingeniously conservative. The merit of the old system was that it
gave us some understanding of the nature and interconnection of
truths. The demerit was the inadequacy of the implied methodology of doing physics by deduction. So Leibniz grafted a new
methodology on to the old theory of demonstration. Demonstration was formerly the key to both ontology and method.
Leibniz restricts it to the former. It is turned into the theory of
formal proof. In the old tradition only universal propositions
are subject to demonstration. In the new practice, only what we
now call pure mathematics fits this model. But Leibniz, making
proof a matter of ontology, not methodology, asserts that all true
propositions have an *a priori* proof, although in general human
beings cannot make those proofs. This is to resolve the open
question as to the nature of truth. Hence his careful distinction
between finite and infinite proofs, the importance of form over
content, and all the rest of Leibniz's rendering truth 'mechanical'. The universal characteristic, you will recall, 'renders truth

[1] 'On the radical origination of things', 23 Nov. 1697, *P*. VII, 305.

stable, visible, and irresistible, as on a mechanical basis'. The new science that was not *scientia* had made truth totally unstable. The concept of formal proof was intended to restore the balance.

The ingenuity of Leibniz's eclecticism shows itself in another direction. The Universal Characteristic, as I have said, was to be the vehicle of finite deductions and of probability calculations of inductive logic. Whereas demonstration is the tool of what was traditionally called knowledge, probability, in medieval times, pertained to a quite different realm, opinion. The low sciences of alchemy and medicine are the artisans of opinion and the forgers of probability—or so I argue at length in a forth-coming book, *The Emergence of Probability*. Those thoroughly alien hermetical figures of the Renaissance did more: they actually engendered a concept of inconclusive evidence derived from facts, as opposed to testimony. The high sciences related to experience in a hypothetico-deductive or one might say 'Popperian' way. That is, they concerned themselves with the deductive connections between experienced effects and conjec-tured causes. The low sciences were too inchoate for that, and created what, in recent times, has been called probability and induction. Leibniz puts the antique theory of demonstration into the realm of ontology. Finite demonstrations become the topic of mathematics, now rendered formal. Architectonic reasoning is his version of the hypothetico-deductive method. Inductive logic is the rationalization of what Bacon dismissed as mere empiricism. The vehicle for all these parts of methodo-logy is the Universal Characteristic. It is a vehicle that cheerfully carries finite proofs and calculations of probability, and yet is a coarse and inadequate mirror of the very nature of truth, the infinite proof.

Carnap and Popper have recently re-enacted the tension between Leibniz's inductive logic and his architectonic reason-ing. My topic today is proof, not probability. I claim that the concept of formal proof was created in the time of Leibniz to overcome quite specific breakdowns in traditional ontology. The Cartesian concept of anti-proof has the same origin. These concepts were devised, almost unwittingly, to fill a vacuum. We still employ those concepts but live in a vacuum that those concepts cannot fill. Consider the sterility of modern philosophy of mathematics—not the collection of mathematical disciplines now called the foundations of mathematics, but our conflicting theories of mathematical truth, mathematical knowledge, and mathematical objects. The most striking single feature of work on this subject in this century is that it is very largely banal. This is despite the ample fertilization from the great programmes and discoveries in the foundations of mathematics. The standard textbook presentations of 'Platonism', constructivism, logicism, finitism, and the like re-enact conceptual moves which were determined by an ancient and alien problem situation, the disintegration of the concept of *scientia* and the invention of the concept of evidence culminating in the new philosophy of the seventeenth century. We have forgotten those events, but they are responsible for the concepts in which we perform our pantomime philosophy.

Take, for example, the most seemingly novel, and also the most passionately disparate of contributions, Wittgenstein's *Remarks on the Foundations of Mathematics*. He invites us to destroy our very speech, and abandon talk of mathematical truth and knowledge of mathematics and its objects. We are asked to try out language in which mathematics is not 'true', our discoveries are not 'knowledge' and the 'objects' are not objects. Despite this fantastic and perplexing attempt to get rid of all these inherited notions, Wittgenstein ends up with a dilemma that is essentially Leibniz-Cartesian. On the one hand he suggests, in quite the most radical way, that mathematical 'truth' is constituted by proof, and on the other he is obsessed by just the intuitions that so impressed Descartes. Hardly anyone thinks he has achieved a synthesis of these notions. There is a reason for this. He rejects that antique tryptich, truth, knowledge, and objects, but works in the space created by that earlier period, and is driven to employ the concepts created then for the solution of quite other problems, and which are fettered by their need to solve those other problems. The 'flybottle' was shaped by prehistory, and only archaeology can display its shape.

PRE-ESTABLISHED HARMONY VERSUS CONSTANT CONJUNCTION: A RECONSIDERATION OF THE DISTINCTION BETWEEN RATIONALISM AND EMPIRICISM[1]

By HIDÉ ISHIGURO

THE grouping of European philosophers of the seventeenth and eighteenth centuries into rationalists and empiricists seems to me to be unfortunate and unhelpful. It suggests that there are two self-contained mutually incompatible sets of views, which are clearly demarcated and based on opposing principles: one claiming that the source of all substantial truths about reality is reason; the other claiming that all knowledge derives from experience. To divide these thinkers into Continental rationalists and British empiricists is even more misleading. It suggests that the grouping of people with opposing sets of beliefs and theories coincided with their nationalities.

Not only did thinkers like Descartes, Spinoza, and Leibniz take great interest in the experimental sciences of their day, they also thought that the data we obtain from our senses played an important role in the formation of our knowledge of the world.[2] On the other hand, as J. MacIntosh has pointed out, Berkeley went so far as to write that intellect and reason are alone the sure guides to truth,[3] and even Locke, who proclaimed that all our knowledge comes ultimately from the senses, defended a theory of knowledge in which an indispensable role is played by elements which, as many have pointed out, cannot be derived

---

[1] In writing this paper I profited from comments on an earlier version made by David Wiggins and by my colleagues, Myles Burnyeat, John Watling, and Richard Wollheim.

[2] This has been argued in a convincing way by others. See, e.g., R. M. Blake, 'The role of experience in Descartes' Theory of Method', *Philosophical Review*, 38 (1929), and E. M. Curley, 'Experience in Spinoza's Theory of Knowledge', in *Spinoza*, ed. M. Grene, p. 25. For Berkeley's views on the importance of reason see J. J. MacIntosh, 'Leibniz and Berkeley', *Proceedings of the Aristotelian Society*, 1971. It can be seen, however, that I do not agree with much of what he says on Leibniz on causation.

[3] Berkeley, *Siris*, p. 264.

from sense–experience. We will see that the same can be said of Hume's theories.

What I would like to draw your attention to today is the view of causation developed by Leibniz, who is often thought to be the rationalist philosopher *par excellence*. His views on causation are widely misunderstood. A proper understanding of them will go against the received view of the contrast between rationalism and empiricism. Three points in particular will be important.

The first is the considerable similarity between Leibniz's theory of causation, namely the doctrine of pre-established harmony, and the opinion of Hume on this subject so familiar to the British philosophical public—in contrast, for example, to the views of Descartes or Locke. We shall see that the experiential evidence for pre-established harmony is not different from the experiential evidence for constant conjunction.

Second, by examining how Leibniz linked his views on causation with the concept of the nature of things and of force, we shall see, despite all their similarities, the ultimate difference between Leibniz's views and those of Hume. It is impossible, however, to do justice to this difference in terms of the ordinary stereotypes of rationalism and empiricism. It involves Leibniz's belief in the possibility of *a posteriori* knowledge of real essence, which Locke thought unknowable.

Third, it should become apparent how Leibniz's views compare with recent theories of causal explanation: especially theories related to counterfactual conditionals and nomological deductive theories. I hope that the comparison will suggest how misguided are the standard criticisms of Leibniz's account of causation.

1. *Hume and Leibniz*

It is well known that Leibniz denied the philosophical doctrine of causal interaction. It is seldom understood what it was that he was denying. Russell, for example, wrote, that, according to Leibniz, 'nothing really acts on anything else'.[1] But what is the difference between really acting on something and seeming to act on it? Many people seem to have thought that Leibniz's denial of causal interaction amounted to the claim that there was no connection between what happens to one thing and what happens to other things. If this were a correct interpretation, it would be a mystery that Leibniz was always interested in the investigation of the laws of dynamics and the correct mathematical

[1] *The Philosophy of Leibniz*, p. 93.

formulation of them. He wrote several treatises on dynamics. His disagreement with Descartes and with Newton about the laws of dynamics never concerned the question whether there exist laws stating the interconnection of material things. They related only to how the laws should be formulated. Noticing law-like regularities was what made nature comprehensible to men. As Leibniz writes, the central concept of dynamics was that 'there is always a perfect equivalence [by which he means equality of energy] between the full cause and the whole effect'.[1] Leibniz is far from denying the existence of conditions or events that are causes and conditions or events that are effects. Nor does he deny the importance of the causal explanation for macroscopic physical things. As far as macroscopic physical things were concerned his views were very much in the spirit of the mechanism of his time. As he says, 'But in phenomena everything is explained mechanically and so masses are understood to impel each other'.[2]

Some philosophers have said that Leibniz's denial of causal interaction concerns only monads, which were, strictly speaking, the only individual substances for Leibniz, and therefore has nothing to do with the causal explanation of physical events, which are according to Leibniz phenomena. It must be recalled, however, that Leibniz first expressed his denial of causal interaction in an article concerning the mind-body problem; and in his discussion on causation he repeatedly refers to the relationship between mind and body, as well as to that between the mind and phenomenal changes in the outer world. The body is an aggregate according to Leibniz—an infinite complex machine—and also something we identify as a spatial, extended thing, i.e. a phenomenon. Leibniz even wrote that his system of pre-established harmony has the advantage of conserving what he calls the 'great principle of physics', the inertial laws of bodies, in its full rigour and generality.[3] The scope of the doctrine is not as limited as these critics have supposed.

[1] Reply to Abbé Catelan in *Nouvelles de la République des Lettres*, Feb. 1687.
[2] Letter to de Volder, 1703. *G* II, p. 250; *L*, p. 529. (*G* is Gerhardt, *Philosophische Schriften*, vols. I–VII. *L* is *Leibniz's Philosophical Papers*, ed. Loemker, published by Reidel.)
[3] 'Consideration on Vital Principles and Plastic Natures', 1705. *G* VI, p. 541; *L*, p. 587. In a letter to Arnauld he reflects that his denial of causal interaction between corporeal substances may be even more surprising than his denial of causal interaction between monads, since action of one body on another may appear so undeniable. Letter to Arnauld, 14 July 1686. *G* II, p. 58; *L*, p. 338.

Many popular commentators have claimed to be puzzled by an analogy, which Leibniz made in the *Monadology* for a popular audience. He says that monads have no windows; they are like mirrors which reflect the rest of the universe. But there is no puzzle here. Leibniz does not use the contrast between the mirror without windows and a thing with windows to point to an esoteric fact hidden behind appearances. His concern is with a familiar recognizable truth. The analogy reminds the reader of something he should already know about if he is to think about the problems without preconceived ideas: viz. what is involved in causal explanation. When we think that a moving billiard ball causes another ball to move by impact, we do not need to suppose that something goes out of one ball and into another. The motion of one ball does affect the motion of the other ball. But it is the velocity, motion, and direction of *each* ball that changes. The denial that there is something literally transmitted in these causal transactions is the point of Leibniz's analogy of windowless monads. Whereas we do think of a reflection in a mirror as a typical case of a state caused by external events. Corresponding to the changes in the vicinity of the mirror, there will be changes in the image on the mirror— but not because a bit of the external world enters the mirror. The (intact) mirror by its (very) own nature, changes its state in a manner corresponding to the change outside. Of course, light waves of certain kinds travel to the surface of the mirror. But they do not go into it. If anything, Leibniz's analogy of the mirror shows not only that he believed in the existence of what we would now call causal relation; it shows that he thought it much more far-reaching than is normally assumed. Every entity has a causal relationship with everything else in the universe.

I therefore think it is misleading to write as many have done[1] that according to Leibniz there is no such thing as causal inter-action since each substance is separately 'programmed' for the whole of its history. Each substance has its nature. Given that the substance finds itself in a universe with other things, this nature programmes its history. The nature of the substance is such that the substance will be affected by other things, in a specific way, and is such that the substance will affect other things in a particular manner. The nature of the monad also determines the nature of aggregates of which it is a constituent, and determines how the aggregate is affected by other aggregates. Leibniz writes, 'Who would deny that a substance is modified

[1] e.g. N. Rescher, *The Philosophy of Leibniz*, p. 83.

through the effect of another substance, for example, when a body is thrown back by an opposing obstacle?'[1] Leibniz goes on to say that we shall, therefore, have to use the concepts of *both* bodies in order to know distinctly the recoil of one of the bodies. He, nevertheless, is careful to add that the recoil is only a mode of that body—it is not as if something alien to the body has come into the body, like a disembodied force, as if from a window, to make it recoil. It was the very nature of that body, with its particular mass and elasticity, to recoil the way it did, given the impact of the other in those particular circumstances.

Now, although the physical objects which we perceive were, according to Leibniz, phenomena of aggregates, interacting with one another by collision and impact, Leibniz did say of monads, which make up these aggregates, that he did not 'admit any action of substances upon each other in the proper sense since no reason can be found for one monad influencing another'.[2] We must, however, give an interpretation of the denial of action 'in the proper sense' between substances, which is compatible with his theories of nomic regularities between phenomena of aggregates. A helpful way is to see what Leibniz was opposing.

The doctrine of causal interaction which Leibniz rejected is not a doctrine of what we today mean by cause and effect. It was a doctrine which was in traditional scholastic textbooks of his time and one which had slipped without much resistance into the vocabulary of the Cartesians and the new physicists: the doctrine of influx.[3] According to this view, when A interacts with B, a form or a quality or a mode which A has, passes from A to B. Thus, if a hot metal bar, A, heats a cold metal bar, B, the heat which was in A is said by the view Leibniz was attacking to move from A to B. If a moving object A collides with another object B, which is at rest and moves it, then the motion of A is said to be transferred from A to B. But Leibniz thought that this theory entailed an absurd idea—the idea that qualities can be detached from substances. Thus, in the passage of the *Monadology*,[4] where Leibniz asserts that monads have no windows

---

[1] Letters to de Volder, July 1701. *G* II. p. 226; *L*, p. 524; *Leibniz: Selections*, ed. Wiener, p. 169.

[2] Letter to de Volder, June 1703. *G* II, p. 251; *L*, p. 530.

[3] Suarez's definition of cause was 'what flows being into something else'. Suarez (1548–1617), *Disputationes Metaphysicae*. For Leibniz's fierce criticism of this view see Preface to an edition of Nizolius, 1670. *G* IV, p. 148; *L*, p. 126.

[4] *Monadology* § 7 *G* VI, p. 607; *L*, p. 643.

through which anything could enter or depart, he explains that
this is so because 'accidents cannot be detached from substances
and march about outside of substances as the sensible species of
the Scholastics once did'. Leibniz is not saying that the Scholastics, nor his physicist contemporaries, put forward a doctrine
of detached accidents. He is saying rather that the Scholastics'
talk about the transfer of forms or the Cartesians' talk about the
exchange of motion, if taken literally, commits them to such a
doctrine. For example, Suarez has defined 'cause' as 'what flows
being into something else'. But what is it to flow being? Leibniz
remarks that even the [syntactical] construction of this phrase is
inept since 'flow' (*influere*) is used by Suarez as a transitive verb,
whereas we only understand its use as an intransitive verb.
(What is it that does the flowing? And what is the 'being'? Is it
another substance or an accident?) Leibniz concludes that this is
a barbarous and obscure definition. For 'flow' is only to be
understood metaphorically, and the definition is more obscure
than the concept of cause which it defines.

But is Leibniz right? We do say, for example, when a physical
body A collides with another body B, that there is a transfer of
momentum. We must realize, however, that this is a metaphorical
expression. What we mean by this is that there is a correlation
between the decrease of momentum of body A and the increase
of momentum of body B, and that a certain conservation principle is observed. We do not mean that any transfer really takes
place.

What could transfer themselves? Are they substances or
qualities? Let us follow Leibniz's query. If the mind and body
are substances then 'it is impossible', Leibniz says, 'to conceive
of material particles or of species or immaterial qualities which
can pass from one of these substances into the other'.[1] How can
a material particle get detached from the body and then pass
into a mind which is not extended, or how could an immaterial
quality—say intelligence—get detached from the mind and
pass on to a material body? It is evident in the case of mind and
body, which are supposed to be different categories, that nothing
that belongs to one category, whether it be bits of the substance
itself or the attributes peculiar to the substance, can transfer
itself to the substance of another category. The difficulty remains,
however, even between causes and effects, which are events
belonging to the same category.

[1] 'Second Explanation of the New System', *G* IV, pp. 498–9; Wiener,
p. 118.

There are then two quite distinct points Leibniz was making in his denial of the traditional doctrine. Leibniz's first point is that to think of free-floating attributes or forms moving from one thing to another is nonsense whether this be between things of different categories or of the same category. Secondly, he holds that to explain causation as *requiring* particles to move from one thing to another leads one to an infinite regress. Transfer of particles does often happen between aggregates. As we will see, Leibniz believed that parts of all bodies are changing continuously. Understanding the pattern of motion often makes us see why certain corresponding changes happen in bodies. But we cannot go on explaining *why* these constituent particles move, by further exchange of particles. (It may be pointed out that Quine, together with many contemporary physicists, has said that causality is the flow of energy. But again we must be careful what is meant by 'flow'. That the propagation of energy can be expressed by wave equations does not mean that we can say of the energy, which is said to flow, that it is the same energy which moves from one place to another, in the way in which we can talk of the same water flowing from one place to another. We are merely talking about the quantity of energy at each contiguous place.) And transfer must be excluded between the simplest entities. By definition, the simplest units, be they Leibniz's monads or the fundamental particles (if contemporary physics admits such ultimate fundamental elementary particles), are not made up of further particles. So not all nomic regularities —nor all of what we call cause and effect—can be explained in terms of exchange of constituent particles, if one accepts as Leibniz did that there are ultimate simple entities.

So much for what he was denying. What was he affirming? We believe we can understand many phenomena. We do give causal explanations of what happens and we predict what will happen, often successfully. Now, we may believe, as, for example, Professor Anscombe has done, that our concept of causation comes from that of derivation, which can be immediately grasped; i.e. that we often perceive that one thing causes another, by simply grasping that the latter derives from the former, prior to any idea of regularity or necessitation. Or we may believe that our causal notions are dependent on something else. Leibniz was of this view, despite the fact that he was quite clear that this something else was not 'influx'. It was, therefore, necessary for him to give an account of what we call cause and effect in a way which does not require exchange of particles or qualities. In this way Leibniz arrives at a view which is very close in certain respects to that which David Hume was to express just over half a century later. Leibniz asserts that 'what we call causes are in metaphysical rigour only concomitant requisites'[1] (*quae causas dicimus esse tantum requisita comitantia in metaphysico rigore*). Compare Hume's claim in the *Treatise* that 'the relation of cause and effect totally depends on the constant conjunction of objects'.[2] Hume even goes so far as to define a cause in the *Enquiry* 'to be an object, followed by another, and where all the objects similar to the first are followed by objects similar to the second', or in other words where, if the first object had not been, the second never existed.[3] In this definition, which is *one* of at least two quite different definitions of causation which Hume gives in both the *Treatise* and the *Enquiry*, Hume is saying that a cause and effect are concomitances, and that the cause is a requisite for the effect: but that is exactly what Leibniz says. Notice that Hume's definition here (unlike his other definition) is not an epistemological one. He is not saying that constant conjunction of impressions constitutes causation, or that regular observation of conjunction of objects makes causation; he is not even saying that all the objects similar to the first have in the past been followed by objects similar to the second. Since causes and effects are said to be objects, they can exist even without being observed. What Hume is saying is that even when cause and effect *are* observed, no further necessary link between them can be observed.

Similarly, half a century before Hume, Leibniz had asserted that for causality the only thing one need require, and the only thing one can directly observe, is concomitance or the harmony itself. In other words, what one observes in observing a harmony is nothing other than the constant conjunction of which Hume was to speak. In a letter to the Dutch physicist de Volder, Leibniz recounts the reply he made to a French Jesuit, Tournemine, who approved of his doctrine of the pre-established harmony—as it explained well the agreement we perceive, for example, between the mind and the body—but said that he still wanted to know the reason for the union between the two. Tournemine claimed the union was different from the agreement. Leibniz replied that this metaphysical union '. . .which the

---

[1] 'First Truths', *c.* 1680–4. Couturat, *Opuscules et fragments inédits*, p. 521; *L*, p. 269.

[2] *Treatise of Human Nature* (Selby-Bigge edition), p. 173.

[3] *An Enquiry concerning Human Understanding*, Section VII, Part 2, p. 76.

scholastics assume in addition to their agreement, is not a phenomenon . . . there is no concept and therefore no knowledge of it'. It follows that no reason can be given for it.[1]

Leibniz criticized Locke's definitions of cause as well as the traditional view. According to Locke, cause is that which produces any simple or complex idea and the effect is that which is produced. Not only did Leibniz find in Locke's talk confusion between an idea and what it is an idea of; even if we allow cause to be what produces an event or a change in the object, the explanation is empty. As Leibniz writes, 'in saying that efficient cause is that which produces . . . you make use only of synonyms'.[2] This was a point that Hume was to raise, in almost the same words, in his *Treatise*.[3] Leibniz then was not denying causation when he rejected the metaphysical doctrine of causal interaction. He tried to clarify what his denial amounts to and writes, 'Just as a Copernican can talk truthfully of the rising of the sun . . . I believe it is very true to say that substances act upon one another, so long as one understands that one is the cause of the change in the other as a consequence of the laws of harmony'.[4]

Nothing which Leibniz says leads to the view that the cause has temporally to occur before the effect. It is even easier to establish regular concomitance between two kinds of contemporaneous events. Indeed, many of the examples of concomitances that Leibniz uses are contemporaneous ones. Thus, in so far as Hume was to insist on the temporal precedence of cause in his elaboration on causation, there is a difference between what Leibniz says on concomitance and what Hume was to say on constant conjunction.

We will see, however, that when events are not contemporaneous, Leibniz claimed that whatever is the cause must precede the effect. This is related to an important difference between Leibniz's view and that which Hume explicitly stated at least in the *Treatise*. And here I come to the second point of my lecture: by linking the concept of causation to the nature of objects and to the concept of energy Leibniz succeeds in giving an objective realist basis to the causal concept, despite the fact that he thinks that causality consists only of a certain kind of concomitance.

[1] Letter to de Volder, 19 Jan. 1706. *G* II, p. 281; *L*, pp. 538–9.
[2] *New Essays Concerning Human Understanding*, II, 26, § 1.
[3] *Treatise*, Part III, Section 4, p. 157.
[4] 'Explanation of the New System of the Communication of Substances', 1695. *G* IV, p. 495.

2. *Concomitance and the nature of things*

Regularity or regular concomitance is what makes nature comprehensible. The necessity of this concomitance is not produced by any propensity of the mind such as that which comes from habit. The mind may well acquire such propensities and certain expectations, some of which may be right and some wrong. But the fact that certain perceptions follow each other is itself based on concomitance between changes in the external world and changes in one's perceptions. If the regularity of the changes in the external world have grounds at all, be they causes and effects or two different effects of the same cause, it comes from the nature of things in the external world. Change from night to day is due to the rotation of the earth. The fact that *we observe* night followed by day repeatedly is no ground for claiming that we will continue to have similar experiences. If we understand that the regular change in our perception comes from a regular change in the outside world, in this case the earth, and, if we understand that this rotation of the earth comes from its stable nature, then that is the basis for expecting our experiences to continue. Leibniz speculates on what he calls the great analogy between the earth and the magnet. And, just as magnetism depends on the nature of the matter of the magnet and the matter of the things attracted to it, so regularities in nature come from the nature of things.[1] Leibniz does not think that necessity is a quality of an object, or even a perceivable quality of a relation, any more than Hume did. But it is not something conjured up by the mind. It is a feature of certain regularities in nature, which is based in turn on the nature of things.

Think of the example mentioned above of two bars, one hot and one cold, standing adjacent to one another. Eventually, the bars would be of the same temperature. Even if the size of the bars and the initial temperature of the two bars were fixed, the time it would take for the two bars to become the same temperature would differ enormously if the bars were made of copper, or if they were made of porcelain. This entirely depends on the nature of copper or porcelain itself. If it were just a question of disembodied heat travelling from one bar to another, there would be no difference in the time required.

In one of his early works, Leibniz had defined the nature of a

---

[1] Letter to Huygens, Sept. 1692. *GM* II, pp. 141–6; *L.* p. 415.

thing as the cause in the thing itself, of its appearance.[1] When in 1682 Robert Boyle caused a controversy by writing an attack on what he called 'vulgarly received notions of nature', and suggested that the vague term 'nature' be replaced by the more precise term 'mechanism', Leibniz wrote a paper called 'On Nature itself, or on the inherent Force and Actions of created Things'.[2] According to Leibniz, any particular mechanism can be understood by something further—the inherent force which endures in the things that enter into mechanical laws. Thus, it is not correct to say that nature is the mechanism of bodies. The force of energy is in the bodies permanently, even when they are at rest. Force is not identical with the mass spoken of by his physicist contemporaries, which was something passive. Force is active in that it corresponds, Leibniz says, to the law which gives the series of states of the body in motion—given what is happening in the rest of the universe. There is no inconsistency in asserting that everything happens mechanically in nature: that is, according to certain mathematical laws that express a relation, which holds between a plurality of things, and saying at the same time that everything acts according to its own nature.

Let us remind ourselves of Leibniz's own formulation of the doctrine of pre-established harmony. He gave this name to his system of explanation comparatively late in life, and talks of this doctrine by this name only in connection with the mind–body problem where efficient causes and final causes seem to meet. Pre-established harmony is a system of explanation, which is applicable to all substances, however, and is based on his view, which he espoused very early, about what is involved in all causation, even that involving only efficient causes. (One may compare here the Cartesians, who expressed their doctrine of causal interaction only in connection with the mind-body problem, but never thought that causal interaction operated only between mind and body.) Leibniz says that the harmony or correspondence between the mind and body is not a perpetual miracle, but the effect of the nature of each of them, and is no more nor less miraculous than any regularity between the states of change of any natural thing. It is 'a perpetual wonder', he writes, but 'a perpetual wonder as many natural things are'.[3]

Thus, Leibniz claims that it is true not only of the soul, but of

---

[1] 'An Example of Demonstrations about the Nature of corporeal Things drawn from Phenomena', 1671. L, p. 142.

[2] 1698. G IV, pp. 504–16; L, pp. 498–508.

[3] Leibniz–Clarke Correspondence, Letter V. G VII, p. 412; L, p. 711.

every other real unity that '*everything in it must arise from its own nature by a perfect spontaneity with regard to itself, yet, by a perfect conformity to things without*'.[1] This he calls the doctrine of pre-established harmony. What does Leibniz mean? What would it be for a thing to lack spontaneity with regard to itself? What is added by 'spontaneity'? This is added in order to rid people of the notion that change could happen to things in ways quite unrelated to the nature of the things themselves. Every change, every event that occurs to a thing, expresses the nature of the thing. As Leibniz explained to Pierre Bayle, a thing continues to change when it changes 'always following a certain law . . . And this law of order which constitutes the individuality of each particular substance, is in exact agreement with what occurs to every other substance and throughout the universe.'[2] The acknowledgement of the pre-established harmony then is nothing other than the recognition that things are created with natures such that they behave in law-like regularity in the universe. Although the nature of each substance is different, many substantiating a different set of laws and each substance substantiating even the same laws in different ways, the laws themselves apply to all substances, and thus the concept of 'law' here does not become empty and trivial, as Russell feared.

Leibniz claims that to believe in the existence of the laws of nature is not to believe in the existence of laws disembodied. God cannot create disembodied laws. Substances and laws are fixed simultaneously. In creating a universe governed by law-like regularity, God does *not* carry out two distinct acts of creation. By establishing the laws, God does not merely give us a way of describing things by the extrinsic or contingent relational properties.[3] To say of God that he established laws is, Leibniz insists, to say that he conferred on things some imprint that endures within them. We should not, however, think of this in too pictorial a manner. The physical world with its mass has its laws of nature within it. And this is to say that each thing down to the simplest substance in it acts in accordance with the internal force and laws of its own nature. This is the only fact

---

[1] 'New System of the Nature and Communication of Substances', § 14, 1695. *G* IV, p. 484; *L*, p. 457.

[2] Clarification of the difficulties which M. Bayle has found in the new system. *G* IV, p. 518; *L*, p. 493.

[3] It is not that 'the law had bestowed upon things only an extrinsic denomination'. 'On Nature itself, or on the inherent Force and Actions of created Things', 1698. *G* IV, p. 507; *L*, p. 500.

which is common to things on the macroscopic level, i.e. aggregates, and to simple substances. As he writes, 'For me nothing is permanent in things except the law itself, which involves a continuous succession and which corresponds in individual things to that law which determines the whole world.'[1] In the case of a simple substance, *ex hypothesi* it has no structure. The only way we can specify its nature is to give the law which generates the events it partakes in, in aggregation with other simple substances.

In fact, Leibniz says the foundation of laws of nature is the principle of the conservation of active force or energy and he defended his view against Newton's spokesman, Clark. (Clark had claimed that when soft inelastic bodies collide there is no conservation of energy.) But how can the law of conservation of energy be embodied in individual things? Does this not lead to the view that the momentum of each body remains constant, which is obviously false? No. Leibniz is not committed to such a blatant mistake. What he says is that each thing embodies a law such that the thing acts in correspondence with other things so that *the totality of energy in the world is preserved*. This is not a correspondence by 'fluke', since for Leibniz each substance by its own nature also registers at each moment what is happening to the other things in the world. We can see that the concept of laws of nature is inseparable from the concept of energy. All that we perceive is magnitude, figure, and motion. But we can understand that the nature of matter is not merely extension, for instance, by perceiving that it is not the quantity of motion, which is constant. What we observe is a particular over-all relationship which holds for the plurality of things between direction and quantity of mass. At any instant we can measure the momentum of a thing. This is what Leibniz calls derivative force. By thinking about what we observe we obtain the concept of active force which resides in things. This is what Leibniz calls primitive force, or the nature of the thing, which is the law of the series of the changing momentum of the thing, given the states of the other things.

There are two trains of thought which lead Leibniz to his belief in the inherent active force of simple substance. First is his conviction that action must ultimately arise from something active. Anything that is merely passive, such as Descartes's matter whose essence is extension or a mere plenum, cannot bring about action. On the other hand, Leibniz believed that

[1] Letter to de Volder, Jan. 1704. *G* II, p. 263; *L*, p. 534.

inertia and impenetrability of matter was neither a primary property, nor a property derivable from the extension of matter, but needed to be explained by an active force in the thing itself.[1]

Second, Leibniz thought that the concept of extension was 'incomplete'.[2] In this context he understands by this what we mean by second order concept. Strictly speaking, this paper is not extended and white. It is extended paper that is white. Leibniz had said, as Frege was to say almost two centuries later, that number was a concept which depended on other concepts— sortal concepts. There must necessarily be something numbered. Nothing can be three and apples, though there may be three apples. Leibniz held that extension shares this feature with number and multitude. All extension is an extended something. Leibniz concludes, therefore, that what is extended is something prior to extension, something prior to plurality or repetition. This must be active force. Active force is ascribable even to a simple monad, which, on its own, has no extension.

Now, as is well known, Hume gave two quite different accounts for the necessity involved in causation. On one hand, he wanted to say that the necessary connection between objects, which is part of the idea of cause and effect is *nothing* but our propensity to pass from an object to the idea of its usual attendant.[3] On the other hand, he did say that causation depended entirely on the constant conjunction of objects, and not on the constant conjunction of our perceptions; and necessity seems to be ascribed to the relation of the objects themselves. This is most clear in the *Enquiry*, when in defining cause, he writes that 'if the first object had not been, the second never had existed'.[4] This is clearly a necessary relationship that exists between two objects, quite independent of whether anyone observes it or not. And *that* necessity cannot be explained just by the mind's propensity or custom or any psychological fact as Hume thought, even if it is also a psychological fact that we have an ability to recognize certain patterns and form certain ex- pectations when we have repeatedly encountered causes and effects which hold between objects of certain types. Hume must have been influenced by his reading of Leibniz, when in one passage in the *Enquiry* he acknowledges that we can learn from the succession of our ideas only if there is agreement between our

[1] e.g. Letter to de Volder, Mar.–Apr. 1699. *G* II, pp. 169–70; *L*, p. 516.
[2] Ibid.
[3] *Treatise*, Part III, Section 14, p. 165.
[4] *An Enquiry concerning Human Understanding*, Section VII, Part 2, p. 76.

ideas and objects in nature, and says, 'here then, is a kind of pre-established harmony between the course of nature and the succession of our ideas'.[1]

It is Leibniz's strength to have explained causation in terms of concomitance or conjunction, and yet to have accounted for the necessity of the concomitance in the nature of the objects themselves. This also enabled him to link the concept of cause with the direction of time. He claimed quite clearly in at least one paper that, if one of two states which are not simultaneous involves a reason for the other, the former is held to be prior, the latter posterior.[2] Past states, unlike future states, can leave traces, or generate a process and thus affect future states. These traces or impressions remain in objects; processes go on in the external world, and not only in the mind of the observer. Thus, the temporal precedence of a cause is based on objective grounds pertaining to the external world, not merely on habits of the mind of observers.[3]

It might be thought that this difference between Leibniz and Hume is a simple reflection of the difference between rationalism and empiricism. One can perceive the repeated conjunctions, it may be said, but one cannot observe internal forces or past histories. The problem is not so simple, however. For one thing, Leibniz thought that there were observable differences between physical things, which acted out of the internal force which was enduring in them, and things which could be explained in terms of motion of passive matter. Our view about force is an assumption or a hypothesis, but it is based on our observation.

Leibniz thought that one could assess the probability of such hypotheses empirically. 'Some hypotheses can satisfy so many phenomena, and so easily, that they can be taken for certain . . . a hypothesis of this kind is like a cryptograph, and the simpler it is and the greater number of events that can be explained by it the more probable it is.'[4] There can be no empirical *proof* of a hypothesis for, as Leibniz goes on to say, the same phenomenon can always in principle be explained in several different ways, and, thus, no firm demonstration of the truth of a hypothesis can

[1] Ibid., Section V, Part 2, p. 54. This was pointed out to me by Dr. J. Watling.

[2] 'Metaphysical Foundations of Mathematics', *GM* VII, p. 17; *L*, p. 666.

[3] This claim of Leibniz does not by itself give us any adequate topological features of time. It is compatible with time being discontinuous. For him time is continuous because it is the order of all possible as well as actual states.

[4] 'An Introduction on the Value and Method of natural Science', *L*, p. 283.

be made from the success of a hypothesis. Nevertheless, according to him, empirical data do and must affect the way we accept or reject the hypothesis.

We must also notice that the ways we come to know the nature of macroscopic objects and the nature of simple monads are somewhat different.

(a) Complex objects

Everything that is extended and has parts, be it a clock or an atom of contemporary physics, is a complex aggregate. Leibniz writes that material bodies are almost like a river which always changes water or like the ship of Theseus which the Athenians were always repairing.[1]

In the case of complex objects, Leibniz did think that we can come to an understanding of how force operates by coming to know the structure (or 'contexture') of the object itself and of the changes that are occurring in it. For example, he writes that by coming to know a particular structure of a clock, whether it moves by spring or by wheels, we can understand why a hammer of a clock strikes when a given time elapses.[2] For even if we do not observe any force transferring itself out of the wheels and into the cog, because there is none, we can see how the equal quantity of motion in one is made to correspond to the equal quantity of motion in the other. (We can similarly see how certain electric phenomena correspond to the flow of electrons within a bigger conglomerate of atoms.) Leibniz was not persuaded by Locke that the real essence or real constitution of physical things is unknowable to us.[3] We are, as a matter of fact, ignorant about the constitution of many physical things, just as we have vague confused ideas about the qualities of many objects. But just as we may come to have empirical knowledge of the constitution of the clocks, we may come to have empirical knowledge of the constitution of more minute things. For example, he says, 'it is possible that bodies which are exceedingly subtle and cannot be caught or perceived by sense in one substance can be caught in another'.[4]

Locke had said not only that the real essences of things 'are unknown to us. We cannot discover so much as that size, figure

---

[1] *New Essays*, Bk. II, Ch. 27, § 4.

[2] Ibid., Bk. III, Ch. 6, § 39; Bk. IV, Ch. 6, § 7.

[3] Locke, *Essays Concerning Human Understanding*, III, p. 17.

[4] 'On a Method of arriving at a true Analysis of Bodies and the Causes of natural Things.' *G* VII, p. 267; *L*, p. 174.

and texture of their minute and active parts, which is really in them, much less the different motions and impulses made in and upon them by bodies from without.'[1] He went on to claim that such consideration should put an end to all our hopes of ever having the ideas of real essences. In so far as Locke admits the existence of these real essences—for which he, unlike Leibniz, thinks there is no possibility of empirical knowledge—he is the one who breaks the so-called canons of empiricism.

As will have been clear from what has gone before, Leibniz did not believe that we always *know that we know* the real constitution when we do. But having arguments of his own against the idea that *to know is to know that one knows*, he does not rule out knowledge of the structure of things by which we can comprehend the workings of their inner force.

In aggregates, which are complex processes of simple substances for Leibniz, there are exchanges of entities at all sorts of levels. We will understand the processes better by tracing the exchanges. However, it is not always the case that nomic regularities between complex objects at one level have to be explained by the movement and exchange of entities of a less complex level. What happens when a billiard ball hits another is not like what happens when the nucleus of an atom is split in a synchrotron and an isotope is made. It is not necessary, according to Leibniz, to account for the impact of the billiard ball by the transfer of particles. As I mentioned before, what is standardly called transfer of momentum is not literally a transfer of anything. A billiard ball A's motion does affect the motion of a billiard ball B, but it is the velocity and direction of each ball that changes.

(b) Simple substances

If there were ultimate elementary particles with no parts then we cannot have structural knowledge of them, and causes and effects between events concerning these particles could not be explained by further constituent particles going out of one elementary particle and going into another. We only observe the structure of the aggregate—an atom or molecule or aggregates of atoms—and we observe the corresponding motions of elementary particles within the structures. The same can be said of Leibniz's simple substance. By definition it has no parts and no further constituents. Leibniz concludes, 'Thus the action of one substance on another is not the emission or transplantation of an

---

[1] *Essays*, IV, Ch. 12.

entity as is commonly conceived'.[1] The possibility of fission of
atoms only shows that atoms are not the elementary, or simple,
substances in Leibniz's sense. Leibniz's arguments against explaining causation by emission of particles, unlike his arguments
against detached properties, depend on his belief in the existence
of simple, indivisible substances or ultimate particles (i.e. belief
in a kind of axiom of regularity).

3. *Pre-established harmony and counterfactual truths*

I come now to the third and last point I would like to make today. It is to examine Leibniz's doctrine in the light of recent
views on nomological explanation and on counterfactual
analysis of causation, and try to defend Leibniz's view on the
pre-established harmony from some traditional attacks. We will
then try to see if in any sense we can say that Leibniz's doctrine
is a rationalist view of causation as opposed to an empiricist one.

As we have seen, many philosophers have taken Leibniz's
denial of the metaphysical doctrine of causal interaction and his
doctrine of the pre-established harmony as saying that even if
things *seem* to interact according to dynamic laws, they do so, as
it were, by fluke, each substance acting out a pre-fixed programme, quite independently of whatever happens to other
things. Leibniz is partly responsible for this, since he gives bad
analogies to illustrate his doctrine (like that of the two clocks
which always give the same time because they were set and
wound up in the right way in the beginning. The difficulty about
this analogy lies in the fact that one of the clocks can very well
break down, or begin to lose time, without the other doing so);
he also talks misleadingly about good and bad reasons for God's
actions. Nevertheless, such an interpretation is odd because our
talk of laws of dynamics is normally taken to entail the truth of
certain counterfactuals. To say that the motion of object A after
collision with object B can be explained by the laws of dynamics
is to say, amongst other things, that had the mass of B or the
direction or the velocity of the motion of B at the time of its
collision with A been different then A's motion after the collision might not have been what it was. Leibniz thought in the
same way. Far from believing that one object would behave in a
fixed way, no matter what happened to other things, Leibniz
thought that any difference in the state of other things would
bring about a change to the object. (It seems to me that, if he
errs, he errs in the opposite direction.) He was quite

[1] 'New System of Nature', § 17, 1695. *G* IV, p. 486; *L*, p. 459.

clear about the truths of many counterfactual conditionals, which followed from his commitment to the laws of nature or the pre-established harmony. He writes, '. . . in reality, because of the interconnection of things, the entire universe with all of its parts would be wholly different, and would have been another world altogether from its very commencement, if the least thing in it happened otherwise than it has'.[1]

What then is fixed in an individual when a harmony is pre-established? What is pre-fixed is the nature in each substance to act in accordance with other things, or to act and react to other things not at random but with mutual lawlikeness, whether individually, or in aggregates. In his words, it is 'this mutual agreement, regulated in advance in every substance of the universe'.[2] The pre-fixed nature of magnets and of iron is such that when iron is in the vicinity of a magnet it is drawn to it out of its very own nature in response to the nature of the magnet. Leibniz's own favourite example is perception. The nature of mind (which is a simple substance) is such that spontaneously, by its own nature, it perceives things external to it corresponding to the change in the person's body, which in turn corresponds to change in external phenomena (which are aggregates). This entails the truth of the counterfactual: 'Had the states and changes in the external world been different the perceptual states of the mind would also have been different'.

The introduction of the talk of the pre-established harmony, or pre-fixed nature, allows us, therefore, to give truth-values to certain counterfactuals. This is something which the observation, however repeated, of concomitance does not allow us to do. It does *not*, therefore, make each aggregate and each substance behave independently of other things. On the contrary, it is an attempt to explain each thing as causally dependent on other things *by the very nature it has*. It commits us to accepting the necessity of certain universally quantified conditional propositions in this world, *given the laws of nature that we do have*. A Leibnizian view thus leads to the acceptance of a nomological deductive theory explanation for all cases which do not involve human action (which is said to be inclined by prior states involving reasons and desires but not necessitated). Given a set of antecedent conditions, which is the state of the world at a given

---

[1] 'Remarques sur la lettre de M. Arnauld touchant ma proposition: que la notion individuelle de chaque personne enferme une fois pour toutes ce que luy arrivera.' *G* II, p. 42.

[2] 'New System of Nature', § 14. *G* IV, pp. 484–5; *L*, p. 458.

time, plus all its history up to that time, one can, in principle, deduce the consequent state, by reference to the laws of nature. As in all such theories, Leibniz's doctrine does not enable one to distinguish causes from antecedent conditions or from other effects of the same cause in any clear-cut way. Leibniz would probably not have minded this. What was important for him was not so much to pick out a cause for every condition or state, but to show how comprehensibility was linked with the stable natures of things and the way they change in correspondence with changes in others. This expressed itself as a functional relationship between the state of one thing and the contemporaneous and ulterior states of other things.

An important point about Leibniz's scheme of explanation is, however, that the identification of antecedent conditions cannot be made independently of the identification of the laws of nature. Laws of nature cannot, as we have seen, exist disembodied. For example, the specification of what kind of things exist, carries with it the laws of nature in virtue of which we can distinguish one kind of thing from another. Thus, in creating a world, God does not carry out two distinct acts of creating substances and their aggregates, and creating the laws of nature. To create substances and their aggregates with natures of certain kinds is to create the laws of nature. We must also notice that there is nothing in what Leibniz says that makes it impossible for the laws to be probabilistic or statistical ones. Nor is there anything that prohibits antecedent conditions from including specifications of whether the subject finds itself within a certain vicinity of certain objects, thereby determining their position in what physicists would now call fields.

As I have said, Hume himself unwittingly committed himself also to objective necessity when he realized that his definition of cause as 'an object followed by another, and where *all* the objects similar to the first are followed by objects similar to the second' leads to the acceptance of a counterfactual, which he formulates as 'if the first object had not been, the second never had existed'. But it is Hume who was to fail to give an empirical justification of his *own* concept of cause, at least in the case of open classes of events or objects. For, as many have pointed out since Kant, our propensity to infer in a certain way after repeated observation of conjunction of events in no way justifies the universality of the conjunction.

Leibniz tried to give an intelligible account of the uniformity of the constant conjunction by linking it to the structure of things (which are phenomena of aggregates), this structure being in principle empirically accessible; and to the active force in things.[1] The existence of this force is postulated because it makes sense of observable phenomena. He was very clear that one cannot ask for further links to explain every conjunction. It was not in his opinion an accidental defect on our part as observers that we fail to perceive such links. It was a conceptual or metaphysical impossibility to explain all regularities between objects by further exchange of particles; and it was conceptual confusion ever to explain anything in terms of transference of detached qualities or modes. But this does not lead to the claim that further investigation of the structure of complex objects, or a hypothesis about the nature of simple objects, can never give the grounds for the regularities.

Now, as has often been pointed out, Leibniz writes in many places of the importance of intelligible realms as distinct from sensible realms. But these two realms are not composed of distinct entities which exist side by side. The two realms correspond to what is given to the senses and what, in perceiving the same reality, is understood by using concepts and theories. We cannot have the concept of justice, which belongs to the intelligible realm, without perceiving the needs and desires of men. We cannot have the concept of active force, which pertains to the intelligible realm, without perceiving motion, rest, and direction. As a matter of fact it is not Locke, but the Cartesians, whom Leibniz attacks for being 'content to stop where the sense perceptions stopped'.[2] He believed that they mistakenly thought that extension was the essential attribute of matter and that the quantity of motion is conserved, because they had not tried to understand clearly enough what they perceived.

The realm of the intelligible in reality is not something one can have access to independently of our senses. It corresponds to the way we draw conclusions from and correctly understand

[1] Bas Van Fraassen has raised the following interesting question. Consider two worlds α and β. Exactly the same thing happens in them; but in α they happen in accordance with laws of nature, while in β there are no laws of nature nor any physical necessity, but as a matter of fact things behave exactly as in α. Are they really distinct worlds? Now, for Leibniz, these would only be distinct worlds if in β things behave the way they do because God or some external power is constantly making the things behave the way they do. If not, then β is the same world as α since to assert that the laws of nature exist is nothing more than to say that things behave in a regular way of themselves and β is a world in which *ex hypothesi* things do so behave.

[2] Letter to de Volder, 30 June 1704. *G* II, p. 269; *L*, pp. 536–7.

what we observe. We do not depend on any one sense to obtain information about the external world. Against Locke, Leibniz does insist that it is possible for a blind man to understand what colour is, even if he has no visual data, and hence does not know what it is to experience perceiving colours. But, in so far as we are bodily people and not angels, what we understand about the external world is not independent of what we perceive. For one thing, Leibniz believed, as did Spinoza, that the mind always represents all changes in the body. Thus, if there is any change in the retina or the ear-drums due to the changes in the light waves or sound waves that reach them, these corresponding in turn to changes in objects further away, then the states of the mind change accordingly.[1] We cannot ignore what we perceive. We can merely make better and better theories to fit in to greater and greater numbers of our perceptions.

Is there any point at all in the traditional labels of rationalist and empiricist? (In the account of mathematical knowledge or of ethics there may be important relevant differences which I will not discuss.) So far as our knowledge and theories relating to the external world are concerned, all philosophers traditionally put under either of these labels seem to have thought that experience was necessary but not sufficient. Thus, if empiricism is supposed to be the doctrine that all knowledge of the world comes entirely from sense perception and rationalism to mean the doctrine that knowledge of reality comes from our understanding independently of the data of our senses, both are positions held by no one and better forgotten. Nor do the traditional labels of nominalism and realism help us. Leibniz considered himself a nominalist, and he was undoubtedly a nominalist in the sense of the medieval dispute—i.e. one who does not believe that universals exist in reality independently of things that instantiate them.

There is, however, a different kind of contrast which we can perhaps make to characterize the kind of difference we have found obtaining between Leibniz's and Hume's account of causation. This is the contrast between the attitude of thinkers who believe that, even if ultimately one can only *describe* the concomitant changes which occur within the structure, the understanding of the global structure of things adds to our understanding of the processes or movements of things in it, and thinkers who want to stick to the case-by-case description of the

[1] See, e.g., Letter to de Volder, Mar.–Apr. 1699. *G* II, pp. 171–2; *L*, p. 517.

concomitances. In this sense Descartes, Spinoza, and Leibniz as well as Locke all belonged to the former group whereas Hume and Berkeley seem to belong to the latter.

It is interesting to notice that in eighteenth-century Japan when there was a great debate between medical doctors who followed the tradition developed in China and Japan on one hand and those who wanted to develop the European medicine introduced by the Dutch in the seventeenth century, the traditionalists described themselves as empirical, and as upholding medicine based on experience against the medical doctrine of the Europeans. The traditionalists claimed that medicine must proceed, and can only proceed, by establishing by repeated observation that certain sets of symptoms and certain sufferings can be cured and men made healthy by the taking of certain herbs or the application of certain ointments.

One of the Japanese physicians who defended European medicine in the eighteenth century, Sugita Genpaku, argued that the strength of the European practice of that time lay in the fact that, by a search for the understanding of the anatomical structures and workings of the body as well as of the material components of the medicines, one comes to understand why a particular medicine has a particular effect on a patient and how the cure comes about.[1] I am not saying that he is necessarily right about what European medical science actually does even at the present day. It may also, to a great extent, be based on case-by-case observations of cures and alleviations rather than on any further understanding of the reasons. What is interesting though is that, in so far as Sugita believed that a holistic structural knowledge leads to understanding of the reason why, and holds the view that however descriptive it may be only global knowledge can give real understanding, he reflects the ideas held by Leibniz and others hitherto labelled rationalist.[2] The traditional oriental doctors were much closer in spirit to Hume.

[1] Genpaku, Sugita, *Words of a Mad Physician*, 1775. Sugita did not deny that the traditional Chinese physicians had views about the structure of the body. He nevertheless thought that their views on the matter were very inexact, and that this came about from their failure to link the understanding of particular ailments with the understanding of the exact structure of the body.

[2] The affinity between Sugita's view and that of Leibniz is remarkable. Leibniz even found himself defending the importance of anatomy against the noted physician and chemist of his time, Stahl. The latter failed to attach proper importance to the study of anatomy.

Let us then reconsider the widely accepted distinction between rationalism and empiricism. In recent decades we have seen much discussion about the status of observation terms and theoretical terms. It is now a commonplace to point out that there are no theory-free descriptions of observation, nor any statements of theory that are free of words with meanings impinging on observable phenomena. If we accept this (and I do), the contrast drawn in the traditional manner between rationalism and empiricism becomes even emptier. In its place there is a real contrast to be drawn among philosophers as well as scientists between two types of thinkers: those who believe that the concepts which they use to explain one type of regularity can be understood only by placing the regularity in the context of a general picture of the structure of the universe, and those who merely express and predict particular types of regularity in what is observed and who avoid or reject linking it to any general concept of reality. The latter are interested in the question whether the particular equations work. To characterize this contrast, as is so often done, in terms of a distinction between realism and operationalism is as misleading as are the labels rationalism and empiricism when applied to the seventeenth and eighteenth century. For even the so-called operationalist presumably believes that the equations express a certain correlation between the commonly observable phenomena or measurements of an external world, which *exists* independently of us even if the measurements are relative to our methods of obtaining them.

The important problem here is whether, without a theory or hypothesis about the whole, one refuses to be satisfied by equations or descriptions of particular types of regularities of observable data, or holds that one should be content with piece-meal descriptions and the mathematical expression of different kinds of regularities. This is not a difference of attitude about quantities of information but about the nature of concepts: about how globally concepts need be or need not be interconnected.

Global theories, like conspiracy theories, perhaps need to be resisted. Precisely because of the temptation we have to build models to explain away whatever we observe, there is a purist satisfaction we feel in refraining from going beyond codifying regularities of particular kinds. (From the original Buddhists who stuck to the description of the suchness of concrete things and their law-like changes, to Paul Valéry who wrote that 'the problem of the totality of things . . . comes from the most naïve of intentions',[1] we see the mind of people anxious to avoid the self-deceiving solace which the appeal to hidden meanings and global theories often bring.) We have seen that Leibniz likened a theorist to a cryptographer. But when people claim to see every-where signs, clues, and confirmation of their own facilely built models and weary us with their self-indulgence and banality we cannot help but be drawn to the dry elegance of self-imposed particularism.

Perhaps only those who are interested by temperament in a wide variety of particular areas of observation, and are rigorous in developing theories to explain the data in each particular area, can allow themselves the luxury of the attempt to make a global theory. Leibniz not only denied that his philosophy constituted a unitary system, he developed and interested him-self in many theories for their own sake, not *because* they linked up with his philosophical doctrines or other areas of investi-gation.[2] The doctrine of pre-established harmony (like Leibniz's other theories on probability, or on infinitesimals) is the creation of a mind insatiably interested also in *a posteriori* knowledge of various phenomena. It is a theory in which the concepts of laws of nature, of the nature of individual substances, of force, and of the direction of time are all intricately linked; it is a global theory but one which tries to account in a unified way for the nature of particular explanatory theories, carefully worked out, which are based on observation.

[1] Paul Valéry, 'Au Sujet d'Eureka' in *Variété*, p. 137.

[2] Think of his invention of differential calculus, his interest in probability theory, palaeography, the building of computer machines, hydraulics, law, deontic logic, educational reform, etymology, etc.

TIMES, BEGINNINGS, AND CAUSES
By G. E. M. ANSCOMBE

PHILOSOPHICAL theses sometimes suffer damage from too much success. For reasons of his own the philosopher makes some general diagnosis. As it might be: that all logical truths are tautologies. He creates such conviction that his statement gets to be taken, not as a substantive claim, but as in some way true by definition. Such an over-success happened to Hume's observation that a causal relation is not a matter of logical necessity by which, given the cause, the effect must follow. This got such a hold that it is sometimes argued that some objects (I follow Hume's usage of 'object') cannot be causally related, just because there is a logical necessity of the one, given the other. In this way Hume's substantive philosophical thesis has come to be seen as if it had been a partial definition. I don't think that that was his intention. True, he would have rejected counter-examples. But he would have argued against each specifically. Certainly making a definition out of his diagnosis is an uninteresting move.

Now here is a seeming counter-example, at least on widely accepted views. Friction produces heat. What at first sight could be a better illustration of Hume's own thesis? For couldn't you imagine it producing cold instead? But now we are told that heat is a state of increased excitation of molecules. Well, given that the molecules go on existing—and unless they do how can there be friction? for things would crumble away at the mere attempt to rub them together—given that they do go on existing, how then can they fail to be in a state of increased excitation from friction? For that is the rapid motion against one another of two juxtaposed surfaces; hence there will be a mixture of molecules of either object in some places and this must involve a lot of extra banging of molecules upon one another.

So if that account of heat is right, this will be a counter-example to Hume's contention that the ideas of cause and effect are evidently distinct and that 'the power by which an object produces another is never discoverable merely from their idea'.

For the ideas of friction and heat apparently turn out not to be totally 'distinct'. Are they then not to be *called* an example of cause and effect? That would be the move marking the over-success of Hume's thesis—a stultifying move. Or are we to say that even if heat is increased molecular excitation, the idea of heat is not the idea of increased molecular excitation?—but Hume thought it was the objects that were cause and effect that could always, without absurdity, be supposed to occur one without the other. Here we stumble on the problem of description, which offers us difficulties in formulating Hume's discovery. It is after all a careless use of words to say 'causal connections are not logically necessary' because causal connections are between things, events, and so on, while logical connections are taken to be between suppositions, or predicates. How then are we to formulate the alleged always non-absurd suppositions? We can always frame descriptions of particular causes and effects, which *are* logically connected.

Hume himself avoids this difficulty. He puts the matter like this: where we have a beginning of existence, and a cause of it, there is no contradiction or absurdity in supposing the one to occur without the other. Thus he continues to speak of suppositions—proper subjects of logical relations—without specifying any class of propositions which in his view are always non-contradictory.

But even though we can state his thesis as a generalization without running into the description problem, we cannot be satisfied to leave it at that. Such a general thesis requires not only particular instances illustrative of it, but also a certainty of its being possible to frame the proposition stating the particular instance of it in every case.

To repeat: we can always frame descriptions of particular causes and effects such that the descriptions are logically linked. For example 'Something which caused an explosion occurred' and 'An explosion occurred'. Now that fact surely cannot damage Hume's thesis! Still, how are we to state the thesis with reference to particular cases? It will be useless to say: *some* statements of the occurrence of the cause and non-occurrence of the effect it produced will be non-contradictory. For that sort of move, were it effective, could be used to show that there are no necessary connections of any sort, no necessary relations between propositions or numbers for example. For, just as we can always form a description of a cause and an effect such that the one logically entails the other, so we can always form accidental descriptions of, let us say, mutually entailing predicates, which do *not* entail one another.

The evasive generalization may be put like this: in general, whatever event E is in question, the cause of E might have occurred and E not have occurred. That is not to say 'For every event E this might have been the case: the cause of E occurred and E did not', but rather 'concerning the cause of E, it might have been that *that* occurred and E not'.

That formulation suggests that there is some description (or: are some descriptions) of the cause, and also of the effect, which are not external, artificial, or oblique but which rather simply present the cause, or the effect (in any particular case) in its character just as a happening. Descriptions which convey the physical reality of the thing that happens, and do not get at it by some other means such as 'the event mentioned in such a place', or 'the (prominent) event which took place in such a room at such a time'. 'Friction' will be such a 'physical description', as I shall call it, and so will 'heat'.

However, it may very likely be argued that 'Friction produces heat' gives us no falsification of the Humean principle. For there are both empirical investigation and theory coming between that bare statement 'Friction produces heat', which is the product of the most elementary observation, and the idea that the molecules at the surfaces of the two objects suffer increased excitation when they are rubbed together, which is heat. That is true: but then how are we to understand Hume's thesis? Is it to be taken as saying only that a rudimentary understanding of the objects which are causes and effects will never yield a necessary connection? That so long as we remain ignorant of the nature of things, we will find no logic in the sequence of events? That would not be too impressive. A proper physical statement of the cause will never logically yield a proper physical statement of the effect—that is the thesis. If so, then friction producing heat, on being properly understood, will also be a fair counter-example. It cannot be excluded on the ground that some empirical investigation has gone on before that formulation is reached. For the investigation was into the nature of this cause and this effect.

The description problem is a deep one and I will beg leave to go no further with it here but to assume it solved. Certainly if it can't be solved, Hume's primary discovery was nothing. I believe it was a great one, a great correction of false philosophic assumptions. But also, that it was not true without exception.

I do not myself accept the counter-example I have given, because the explanation of heat seems wrong. At very high temperatures the molecular bond is dissolved—so at best some reformulation is necessary. (And think of the radiant heat in the interior of the sun: how absurd to say that *that* is not heat.)

But here is a genuine counter-example. I find an object in some place and ask how it comes to be there. One partial causal explanation would be that it travelled there from some-where else. Call the place it was at before '*A*', the place where it is now '*B*'; our causal explanation is that it went along some path from *A* to *B*. As opposed, that is, to arriving at *B* from *A* in some other way. And also, as opposed to its coming into existence at *B*. But travelling from *A* to *B* necessarily involves being at *B*—even if only for one point of time.

Suppose our object turned up at *B* after having been at *A*, but without traversing any path from *A* to *B*, then it would be empty indeed to call 'It arrived *at B* from *A*' a cause of its being at *B*. 'It was at *A* before' might state such a cause, but not 'its arriving at *B* from *A*', for that just adds the description of the effect to the description of the cause. Not so 'It travelled from *A* as far as *B* by some path'. That however entails, not indeed its being at rest at *B*, but at least its being at *B*.

Hume wouldn't accept this as a counter-example. But that is because of his—unacceptable—views on space and time. *He* would have divided the journey into two parts: the part up to immediately before the thing was at *B* and the 'contiguous' part in which it was at *B*, and he would have said that at most the first part might be cause of the second. But this requires the absurd notion of the contiguity or strict adjacence of bits of space and time with no points in common. Thus what I call Hume's major thesis about causality hangs together with his atomism, with his rejection of the continuum. It depends on that for its universality. I count it as not universally true, and would say that Hume showed us only that causal relations do not as such involve logical connections of cause and effect. In fact the example of travel is the only kind of counter-example that I know.

Hume is making a substantive claim, then, not a stipulation about what we are to call 'causes and effects'. And the claim seems to be almost universally true. I suspect indeed that it can be faulted only where it is tied up with his views on space and time. It is true that causal properties enter into the definition of substances, so that you might think certain effects resulted of necessity—logical necessity—from the interaction of substances. But you would be wrong in making this inference. A *lusus naturae* is always logically possible. A different melting point may indeed prove this isn't phosphorus; the lump of phosphorus turning into a little bird or a piece of bread would not.

Hume's observation ought to have been a very liberating one. But so far few people have been much liberated, for Hume himself, and almost everybody since, has been anxious to forge some substitute for the chains that he broke—to replace the logical necessity by another one just as universal as it.

I want to discuss a quite distinct doctrine of Hume's, which is often accepted with this one in a single package. I mean his doctrine that his form of a 'law of universal causation', namely 'Every beginning of existence has a cause', has no logical necessity about it.

It is obvious that the doctrines are distinct. Suppose there is a logical necessity about 'Every beginning of existence has a cause'. It would not follow that the connection between any particular cause and its effect involved any logical necessity. For 'Every beginning of existence must have a cause' only says of every beginning of existence that it must have some cause or other, not that there is any given cause that anything must have. Conversely, someone might think that every case of cause and effect, properly stated, involved a logical necessity of that cause's having that effect and/or that effect's having that cause, while not thinking that beginnings of existence had to have causes. (This was McTaggart's view.)

Hume appeared to recognize the distinction of the two questions—but, having once proved to his own satisfaction that 'Every beginning of existence has a cause' is neither intuitively nor demonstratively certain (i.e., as people would say now, is not a bit of logical truth), he 'sinks' the question why we believe it in the question why 'we' believe in the necessary connection of particular causes and effects. Well, I don't believe that quite generally, in *any* sense of 'necessary connection'. We need reason to believe such a thing, and Hume was right in thinking there was none. He was only wrong in thinking that we were under a compulsion to believe it.

Hume's attempted proof that 'Every beginning of existence has a cause' is not a logical certainty is not satisfactory. It goes like this.

As all distinct ideas are separate from each other, and as the ideas of cause and effect are evidently distinct, 'twill be easy for us to conceive any object to be non-existent this moment, and existent the next, without conjoining to it the distinct idea of a cause . . . The separation, therefore, of the idea of a cause from that of a beginning of existence, is plainly possible for the imagination; and consequently the actual separation of these objects is so far possible, that it implies no contradiction or absurdity.[1]

The argument is apparently based on a belief that if we can think of one thing (in this case, a beginning of existence) without thinking of another (in this case, a cause) then the one can occur without the other. In its contrapositive form, 'If there can't *be* one thing without another, you can't *think* of the first without thinking of the second', Hume certainly assented to this general principle, and in this form its absurdity is now generally realized. It is what leads him to say that you cannot think of anything without thinking of it in full particularity. So it may seem odd that the reasoning here, about causes, is so widely believed. The reason is perhaps partly that what Hume is arguing for here is not always sharply distinguished in people's minds from the great major thesis, and partly also that this argument is credited as an argument from imagination to possibility. 'We can imagine a beginning of existence without a cause, therefore there can be a beginning of existence without a cause.' But what interest or value can there be in such imagining? I might as well argue that, because I can imagine circle-squaring, that is possible. It is different when I use the argument from imagination in a particular case of cause and effect. For here it may be clear that I do know what it would be like to establish the occurrence of *this* phenomenon without *this* cause.

Having said this, however, *reculons pour mieux sauter*, so that we may find what is true about the argument. Certainly if we look at a thought as a psychological event, and, by the 'experimental method' as suggested on Hume's title-page, try what we *can* think without what, the argument lacks all force. But suppose we consider a thought, not as a psychological event, but as the content of a proposition, the common possession of many minds. We may then find a way of putting the point. As Aquinas remarks,

Habitudo ad causam non intrat in definitionem entis quod est causatum.[2]

---

[1] *A Treatise of Human Nature*, Bk. I, Pt. 1 Sect. iii.
[2] *Summa Theologica*, I, XLIV, art. 1.

The relation to a cause does not enter into the definition of the thing that is caused.

and so someone may argue that:

Nihil prohibet inveniri rem sine eo quod non est de ratione rei: sicut hominem sine albedine. Sed habitudo causati ad causam non videtur esse de ratione entium: quia, sine hac, possunt aliqua entia intelligi. Ergo, sine hac, possunt esse.[1]

Nothing prevents a thing's being found without what does not belong to its concept, e.g. a man without whiteness; but the relation of caused to cause does not seem to be part of the concept of existent things: for they can be understood without that. Therefore they can be without that.

This strips the argument (as it occurs in Hume) of the damaging experimental premiss about what we can conceive without also thinking of what. Nor is there here an argument from imaginability to possibility. Rather Aquinas is using the idea of the *ratio* (Greek *logos*), which I have rendered 'concept', of a thing.

Thus the argument published by Aquinas goes:

It is possible to understand existents without the relation of caused to cause

∴ That relation does not belong to the concept of existents

∴ They can lack that relation.

Whereas Hume's version goes:

It is possible to conceive an object coming into existence without conjoining the distinct idea of a cause

∴ It is possible to imagine: an object coming into existence without there being a cause

∴ It is possible for an object to come into existence without a cause.

There is a great similarity; an important difference is the idea of the grasp of a concept which gives what is essential to a matter, which we find in Aquinas's argument. (And something like this we have already looked for in our attempt to introduce 'proper physical statements' of the occurrence of a cause and its effect.) This enables Aquinas to avoid the more obviously false or inconsequent bits of Hume's argument. It thus appears to

[1] Ibid.

convey what is acceptable, what has been found convincing, in the suggestions of the passage from Hume.

However, the thing that in Hume's argument is said—as we may now put it—not to involve a relation to a cause is not the thing that is caused, but its coming into existence. So what we have to consider is whether this premiss:

The relation to a cause is no part of the concept of the thing that is caused

entails

A thing can begin to exist without a cause

or again whether we can quite simply justify the assertion:

The relation to a cause is no part of the concept of a thing's coming into existence.

Hume is so satisfied with his own thinking on this question that he deals cavalierly with the only serious argument that he mentions on the other side. It comes from Hobbes; we should be grateful to Hume for bringing it to our notice. As he renders it:

> All the points of space and time in which we can suppose any object to begin to exist are in themselves equal; and unless there be some cause, which is peculiar to one time and to one place, and which by that means determines and fixes the existence, it must remain in eternal suspense; and the object can never begin to be, for want of something to fix its beginning.[1]

This account is a moderately good rendering of the argument as I have been able to track it down in Hobbes (for Hume gives no reference). It may be found in a treatise on Liberty and Necessity; the precise passage is to be found on page 276 of volume 4 of the *English Works of Thomas Hobbes*. It runs:

> Also the sixth point, that a man cannot imagine something to begin *without a cause*, can no other way be made known, but by trying how he can imagine it: but if he try, he shall find as much reason, if there be no cause of the thing, to conceive it should begin at one time as another, that he hath equal reason to think it should begin at all times, which is impossible, and therefore he must think there is some special cause why it began then, rather than sooner or later; or else that it began never, but was *eternal*.

The respect in which Hume's rendering is a bit unfair is that it suggests the absurd picture of an object's hovering in the wings, as it were, and waiting to get on the stage of existence. But I think we would not want to take any notice of that in any case.

[1] *A Treatise of Human Nature*, Bk. I, Pt. III, Sect. iii.

Hobbes's argument is a very interesting one and deserves far more attention than Hume bestows upon it. My interests are not exegetical, so I will not go into the question whether all I see in this argument is really what Hobbes meant. I will only say that consideration of Hobbes's argument led me to the following:

First: in general, the place and time of something's coming into existence are independent of the thing in question. I mean that the place and time in which something comes into existence exist, whether or not that thing, or (in case there is any difference) *such* a thing, does come into existence then and there.

Second: space and time are relative. It is nonsense to think of totally empty space—as Einstein once characterized it, an empty sideless box—consisting perhaps of, or as it were stakeable out as, a set of positions. And it is equal nonsense to think of time as another sort of space (a one-dimensional space) that can be conceived to be empty of existent things and also has its fixed positions for things or events to occupy. Equal nonsense too, to think of the real existence of a space conflated of space and time together, space–time, as an empty space with such a set of positions. It is also nonsense to think of time as a flowing somewhat, as is suggested to the imagination by the phrase 'the passage of time'.

Times are made by changes in things and in their relations, places by the configurations of extended objects and their parts.

From these considerations it follows that a thing's coming into existence at a time and in a place requires at least the existence of other things. That is to say that it cannot be supposed without supposing the existence of other things as well. This, however, is not yet to give what Hobbes's argument seeks to give; the necessity of a cause. For the demand that whatever has come into existence has come into existence at a time is satisfied if we can say: it came into existence a time ago. And similarly for future coming into existence: that will be a time hence. And if, without thinking of past or future, we think abstractly of a thing's coming into existence, and think 'It has to happen, if it happens, at some time', what we are thinking is that it must be a datable event—'in principle', as they say. And that demands that there be other things, but not yet a cause.

Similarly for place. But there is not the same universal necessity for a place, as for a time, of a thing's coming into existence. There would be a difference between the two for the first thing that came into existence. We can at any rate construct that description and reflect on its implications. Grant a first beginning, without an eternal container: 'place' would not apply to it. We might think that the thing's place is no different from its time; we have the time at least as 'for some n, n periods ago', even though there could be no prior or contemporary event to give its birth a time. But 'from here', the spatial ana-logue of 'ago', does not yield much fruit. For how could that—or anything else—be taken as a fixed point of spatial reference by the help of which to assign a meaning to place designations at a time at which nothing fixing that point yet existed? 'Now' of course is not a fixed point of reference either. Nevertheless, in relation to the immense periods of astronomy it is as good as that—one feels no need, for example, to adjust a length of time given as 3×10^{16} secs because the book it was published in appeared some years back! But in any case we would know if we needed to how to add periods to our time of the world as everything gets older. Perhaps, *if* it were on the cards to say how long the universe has existed, the answer would be in some way relativistic (I don't know if this might be so); but there is an *a priori* diffi-culty of a different order about assigning a place to its beginning, i.e. about the idea of any place at all.

An extended object O of any kind coming into existence and being the first thing to do so would make at least two places: an indeterminate one, only specifiable as 'outside' O, and bounded by the surface or limit of O, and a determinate one inside O, also bounded by its surface or limit. If now our object was a uniform sphere, those would be the only two places it would make. But, in supposing and representing such a thing we can construct various geometrically characterized differentia-tions both of the space outside and of the space within. These are possible shapes, partially bounded by the surface or a seg-ment of it, or by lines drawn through points specified in terms of O. But no point on the surface of O will be differentiable from any other and so, unless something of such a shape and relation to the sphere actually comes to be, there will be no difference between potential places defined by congruent shapes and similar relations to the sphere. No difference, I mean, between the places A, or again between B and B, which are severally *represented* as different in the drawing on the facing page. These two distinguished places (namely A and B) would be purely imaginary because *outside* O is indeterminate. For places within the sphere like constructions would give similar distin-guishable sets of indistinguishable places, members of each of which might be illusorily distinguished in a diagram. But the places within (whether distinguishable or not) are not imaginary because there is a determinate whole to suppose divided into parts.

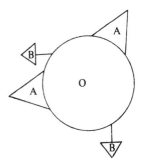

All this is merely to illustrate the principle: No object (or happening), no place. So an object, coming into existence and being the first, or an event which was the first, could not be thought of as coming into existence or happening at a place; it would rather itself bring about the existence of a place. It is the same if it is the universe, the whole world, we are talking about, and we suppose it to have come into existence. Supposing it to have had a beginning means supposing it to have come into existence not out of anything. For if out of anything, that would have already existed and so this event would after all not have been the beginning. I take the universe to be the totality of bodies and physical processes, together with whatever is contained in any manner in the compass of that whole. And so if we take any starting-point by referring to specifiable bodies and processes, the universe will include anything that such things have come out of by way of any sort of development. Thus if the universe had a beginning, it must have come to be out of nothing, i.e. not out of anything. And if we ask 'When and where?' we have to make a difference between the two questions. 'Where?', as we have seen, can have no sense given to it. And so, if it is the whole universe we are talking about, we have to depart from the principle that whatever comes into existence must come into existence somewhere. But to 'When?' the answer will be 'For some n, n periods ago of whatever process we may use to measure the times of the world'.[1] Nothing will then have taken place more than n periods ago.

[1] I will continue to use this form for the sake of simplicity. Imagine a prisoner in a dungeon who keeps a tally of certain recurrent events E, but

Thus in this one case we reject the demand that there be a place. There are no places if there aren't any extended things (including processes): their mutual spatial arrangement makes places. There is no such thing as space (the 'empty sideless box' that Einstein spoke of) *in* which they occur; but the supposition of their occurrence makes us represent an imaginary indeterminate place around them, and that imaginary place is what we call 'space'.

However, we still accept the demand that there be a time when, because the form for giving it is 'so and so long ago'. And so we see that Hobbes's argument does at least suggest my present one. A beginning of existence implies the existence of something other than what begins to exist, even if the implication is satisfied merely by processes within that. If, indeed, we are speaking of the beginning of existence of the universe, that is the only way the implication can be satisfied. To repeat, my supposition of the uniform sphere which was the first thing that began to exist was purely for the sake of certain considerations about place and space. I was not suggesting that we could imagine this: a uniform sphere is the first and only thing to come into existence, and it suffers no development. If someone says he can imagine this, I will consent to him and say I can too: but such imaginings signify nothing in the way of possibility: they are rather bits of symbolism. The point of my uniform sphere could indeed be put otherwise. Let us suppose a uniform sphere. What places can be specified in terms of it? The answer is: inside and outside, and by geometrical construction as I described. Like figures with like relations to it will not determine different places except in terms of something else that exists in spatial relation to it.

All this, however, is not yet to reach Hobbes's conclusion. For the 'other things' involved in a beginning's having a time may be subsequent to it and so not causes of it as Hobbes intended the word 'cause'.

Before turning to this, I will dwell for a little on the temporal expressions which may be used here. 'Before the world began' is a temporal expression which we use if we argue, e.g., 'There cannot have been any things or processes before the world began, out of which it developed'. So it might be said 'before the world

these cease, and he starts another one, of some other recurrent events E^1. Then he might say that he last saw someone 260 E^1's plus 370 E's ago. I don't know whether anything analogous might occur in the matter of the age of, say, the galaxy.

began' would have to designate a time. Again, if the world had a beginning, let it have been n periods ago, i.e. let there have been n and only n cycles or periods of some periodic process which we are assuming as our clock for the universe. We said 'Nothing will have taken place more than n periods ago'. But will not 'more than n periods ago' also designate a time? And similarly for '$n+1$ periods ago': for we may say 'Nothing happened $n+1$ periods ago'.

Also someone may have the following difficulty. If there was a beginning of all things then 'First there was nothing, then there was something', as the lady said in Disraeli's novel. But that requires that 'There is not anything' has been true *then*. And how could that be unless there was a 'then', a time? This is not the difficulty sometimes raised, how a proposition (a sentence) could have been true without existing. For there is no difficulty about that: there are many predicates which do not require the existence of their subject at the time when they hold of it. But must we not here be referring to *a* time—a supposedly 'void time', as Kant called it?

I think that these difficulties about 'then' are all spurious. 'A time' should mean a unit period or a number of unit periods, a long time or a short time; or else a point of time. But 'before the beginning' or (on the supposition of n periods) 'from $n+1$ to n periods ago' cannot designate any length of time, or '$n+1$ periods ago' a point. All that is said is, e.g., that before there were processes there were no processes, i.e. that this is not the case: there were processes before there were processes. We might use the contrast between internal and external negation, and say: We are not saying: 'At t (t being a time designated by "before there were processes") there were no processes', but rather 'Not this: at t there were processes'. Given that n periods is the age of the universe, then 'happened $n+1$ periods ago' is not senseless, however, because of the conceptual possibility of the world's having existed for more than n periods.

If there is a real residual difficulty, it will arise only from the idea of a truth which existed then, if we want to speak of this as opposed to only having a past-tense truth which exists now. We must also assume that a mere truth cannot exist alone: for otherwise there would be no difficulty. For the time before the world would be the time of the existence of the truth that there was no world. However the idea of the existence of a truth and nothing else is unacceptable; because truth is because of the way things are. Note that this is not after all a difficulty about *then*; if we could understand the existence of that truth, the 'then' would offer no difficulty. The truth that there was no world would not be an object or process out of which the world developed, so if it could be supposed to exist it would have existed in a quite different manner from the objects or processes of the world. There would be no length of its duration, nor any temporal differentiation within it. But we cannot accept the mere existence of a truth: that is the difficulty. It was worth considering what would hold if we could, for we see that we would have introduced something whose temporality was altogether different from that of the objects and processes in the universe.

If, then, this is a real difficulty, it can only be solved by postulating some *other* existence or existences which were there before the objects and processes of the universe began, but were not any sort of objects that turned into the bodies and processes of the universe. Remember that I did not explain the 'universe' as 'the totality of all things', as is often done in spite of the dubiousness of such an explanation. I explained it as 'the totality of bodies and physical processes, together with whatever is contained in any manner within the compass of that whole'. This makes it possible to postulate other existences, if there is reason to do so. To describe them as existing before the beginning of the world would not *eo ipso* be to ascribe any temporality to them. For *that*, a mutability in them would also have to be supposed; for without change, duration can mean nothing besides existence itself. Except that, if there are processes going on, and there is an unchanging object which can somehow be compared with those processes, so as to be found or thought of as simultaneous with them, a fictitious distinct idea of its duration arises, as if one could distinguish temporal parts within the 'invariable' object.[1] Now whether anything can be said about such postulated existences, which would be non-temporal or else whose temporalities would at any rate be different from that of our 'clock of the universe', I do not know. And I am uncertain whether the particular difficulty about the existence of truth before the beginning (if there was a beginning) *is* a real or a spurious difficulty. I am only sure that *if* it is a real difficulty, it can be solved only by such a postulate.

An expression that is sometimes on some people's lips is 'before time began'. That might seem quite absurd, and in two different ways. First, it sounds as if time were being thought of

[1] Here I am following Hume.

as that 'equally flowing' thing that Newton spoke of: itself
a process. Second, as 'before' is a temporal expression, how can
we speak of anything as 'before time?' At best it must be a violent
and contradictory metaphor, like 'outside space'. But there is
another understanding of it which neither involves thinking
of time as a process nor invokes a violent metaphor. It may be
understood in the sense 'before *times* began'. *A* time is here to be
understood as a period, 'length of time', an age, or again as a
point. For there to be *times* there must be processes measurable
by some master time-keeping process. A point of time is a
derivative notion, for which it is assumed that the specification
of a length of time between two events, or back or forward from
now, can be precise.

I will now leave these questions, raised by the conception of
a beginning of the world, where it is indeed very difficult not
to flounder and flail about, gasping for breath and uncertain
of talking sense. In all other cases we can accept Hobbes's
assumption that when we conceive of something coming into
existence we conceive it as coming into existence in some place
and at some time. This certainly involves the existence of other
things and so falsifies Hume's contention 'That there is nothing
in any object consider'd in itself, which can afford us a reason
for drawing a conclusion beyond it'.[1] Unless indeed 'something's
coming into existence' is not to be reckoned an 'object' as 'object'
is meant in that dictum—but we have seen that a coming into
existence *is* an 'object' in Hume's usage.

As we have so far understood the existence of other things
to be involved in something's coming into existence, it does not
yet imply the existence of a cause. To this question, then, we
must now address ourselves.

We are to try conceiving the beginning of something without
a cause. It is clear that Hobbes meant really supposing this to
happen, not just forming a picture of it as happening. In discussing Hobbes's argument Hume rather curiously writes as if
what were in question were a proposed existence: 'The first
question that occurs on this subject is always, *whether* the object
shall exist or not: The next, *when* and *where* it shall begin to exist.'[1]
Presumably he meant an existence that one proposes to one's
imagination. But what one ought to propose to one's imagination
is perhaps not the existence of some object, but oneself seriously
judging an object to have come into existence. And here again
Hume is over-easy with his argument from imagination. As we

[1] *A Treatise of Human Nature*, Bk. I, Pt. III, Sect. xii.

have seen, he says ''twill be easy for us to conceive an object to be non-existent one moment, and existent the next, without conjoining to it the distinct idea of a cause'.[1] It is very easy to accept this. Till recently I have done so, I have thought nothing easier than to imagine an object non-existent one moment and existent the next. One can make a picture of it:

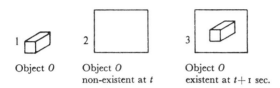

Object *0*   Object *0*   Object *0*
                non-existent at *t*   existent at *t*+1 sec.

and of course one can do this without thinking of a cause. I criticized the suggestion that being able to imagine something-coming-into-existence-without-a-cause proved anything, or was proper material for an argument from imagination. I said that 'something coming into existence without a cause' was a mere title one gave to one's mental picture of something—a rabbit, say, or a star—coming into existence. But I did not then notice that just the same is true of the description 'something coming into existence'.

Following Hobbes, I am to try and imagine—really imagine, i.e. imagine the serious supposition, that some object has come into existence without any cause. Now what reason have I, on this supposition, to assign one time and place to this coming into existence rather than another? Can I just suppose some particular time and place without more ado? Not if what I am to propose to my imagination is that I am truly judging that this object came into existence. I need to envisage myself as having reason to say it came into existence at this time and place and not at any other.

Note that we should not raise this question merely about the object's *being* at a certain place at a certain time. *That* I could have observed to be the case; and if I did, I certainly should not need to make reference to any cause of its being at that place then, in justification of my fixing the object as being here now, there then, and so on. But I have got to suppose the object to have been not existent anywhere one moment, existent in this place the next. How can I do that without supposing a cause which justifies me in judging that *that* was the time and place?

[1] *A Treatise of Human Nature*, Bk. I, Pt. III, Sect. iii.

'Well', says the counsel for the prosecution (of Hobbes):
'Can't you *find* that the object was not in that place at one moment
and that at the next moment it was there? Might you not learn
that this was so from those who observed it? Or, better, may
you not suppose yourself to make the judgement because you
observed this object coming to be at that place yourself?'

But we must notice that there is a difference between coming to
be at a certain place—that is, its coming about that a thing is at
a certain place—and a thing's coming into existence at that place.
So the question arises: granted that it has come about that this
thing is at this place (where it was not before) why is this a
beginning of its existence? Might it not have existed previously
elsewhere and arrived here now?

'Of course it might', the prosecution agrees with some
impatience. 'But it would have to have travelled, i.e. traversed
a path and arrived at this place by approaching it. You could
have been observant enough to exclude that.'

But might it not have arrived from elsewhere without traversing a path from there to here, simply by being first there, then
here?

'No! That doesn't happen. At least, .we are told strange
things about α-particles—but we aren't dealing with them here,
but with familiar macroscopic objects. And such an object
could not be identified with such an object—even of just the
same kind—that had been in another place, unless there was
a spatio-temporal continuity between them.'

But I don't have to make such an identification in order to
justify my doubt. Making such an identification would of course
prove the doubt true, and I would no longer *doubt*. But I am on
the contrary trying to justify myself in saying that this object
came into existence here and did not arrive from elsewhere.
So in such a case my task, it seems, will always be to make sure
that *any* identification of this as this individual with something
that was somewhere else before is excluded. I have got to be
assured both that such objects never behave as we are told
α-particles do and that this one did not travel from anywhere else
in some other form—say as a gas—and resume the form it has
here on arrival. The task is too much for me; and for all I have
a right to judge in the matter, I am forced to conclude that this
object may have come into existence in any place and at almost
any time you care to mention. It seems that there is no experience
which itself *positively* indicates that I have to do with a beginning
of existence here, except indeed that the object is here now and

was not here before. But, that being obviously insufficient, I have got to exclude other explanations of its arrival here. That it came into existence here is apparently to be arrived at by elimination. Or is there any more direct method of judging the question?

The counsel for the prosecution may well be excused if he is goaded by this question into a prolonged exposition and expostulation: '*Of course*', he says 'there is over and over again positive knowledge which shows you that this is a first beginning of the existence of an object—it's hardly ever a question of elimination at all. Take a chair, say, of course it doesn't arrive like an *a*-particle or in any other strange fashion, but you know that because you know how it does come to be; you might have seen the joiner making it out of the wood it was made of, and the wood sawn into planks and the trees cut down, from which it came. Take a baby, it comes from the parents, it grows out of the conjoined sperm and egg. And metals are smelted out of rocks and moulded into pots and rings and other ornaments. Consider the flowers: you yourself took a cutting from a parent plant and planted this one here, and you also started this mustard and cress patch with seeds on a bit of flannel, and you watched it grow. Even without going down a mine we know that the separate lumps of coal were hewed out of the coalface; and we ask a geologist about the process of formation of the coal in the ground. The pudding we are about to eat did not suddenly arrive complete, we know its origin, for it was made in the kitchen out of its ingredients by your sister, you watched her do it. And you know equally well that glass was manufactured out of its ingredients and the clothes you wear were made in a factory out of cloth that was woven out of threads that were spun out of fibres that were, for example, gathered from the cotton plant or teased from the fleeces which had been sheared from sheep. So in a hundred cases we know we can observe beginnings of new items because we know how they were produced and out of what. It is preposterous to claim that no positive actual or possible experience reveals beginnings of existence. We know the times and places of their beginnings without cavil because we understand their origins.'

The defence need make no reply.

The defence rests with the final speech for the prosecution.

THE NATURALISM OF BOOK I OF HUME'S
TREATISE OF HUMAN NATURE
By DAVID PEARS

H UME does three things in the account of the understanding
that he gives in the *Treatise*. First, he argues that certain
concepts and beliefs cannot be explained or justified as the
products of reason operating on sensory experience, and that
they are always misrepresented by philosophers who treat them
in this way. His second step is to consult the vulgar, or ordinary
people, in order to find out how they regard the concepts and
beliefs, and never afterwards to stray too far from their view of
them. Finally, he offers his own theory, which explains and
sometimes justifies them. The first of these three stages is destructive, and it clears the ground for the construction of an am-
bitiously conceived alternative both to rationalism and to naïve
empiricism in the later stages. The alternative is a blend of
sophisticated empiricism and naturalism. The contents of the
mind are all traced back to original experience, which he describes without claiming to be able to explain it, and then he
offers a naturalistic explanation of what the mind does with this
material.

Anyone who works his way through this system wondering
whether it leads to some form of scepticism will be surprised
to find that the outcome is uncertain. This is partly because the
second stage of Hume's account of the understanding is not
purely descriptive, but contains some reinterpretation of the
concepts and beliefs of the vulgar, trimming them to fit the
theory that will be offered in explanation of them in the third
stage. In fact, his attitude towards ordinary people is am-
bivalent: he treats them respectfully when he is criticizing
rationalism, but, when he is developing his own naturalistic
theory, he sometimes finds that they indulge in excesses that
cannot be accommodated within it and, therefore, have to be
trimmed and reduced. Many philosophers hold that his treatment of causal necessity illustrates this tendency. But if such
reductions are legitimate, what are the criteria of scepticism?

Should it be judged by a failure to accommodate the whole system of ordinary people, or only its irreducible core?

Another reason for the uncertainty of the outcome is doubt about what counts as a justification. According to Hume, a concept is justified when it is derived from available experience. But the restrictiveness of his rules of derivation is evidently questionable. However, his own misgivings are mostly concerned with the justification of beliefs, and they arise in two different ways. First, if a belief is the conclusion of an essentially fallible inference, he is inclined to doubt whether the psychological inevitability of that type of inference is a sufficient justification of it, and that is one route to scepticism. Second, when he develops his own naturalistic explanation of fallible inferences, he finds it hard to discriminate between the sensible ones and the foolish ones. This is a fault in his theory, because it ought to have split the class of fallible inferences in a way that at least corresponded to the division into the sensible and the foolish.

He is, of course, aware which of the inferences allowed by his theory are sensible and which are foolish. For when he applies it to ordinary people's beliefs about the objects of perception, he knows that he is giving them the benefit of its lack of discrimination. He interprets the inferences that lead to their beliefs in a way that makes them out to be foolish and flighty, when they are viewed from his Cartesian standpoint, but he explains their origin by pointing out that his theory, or at least his application of it, allows foolish flights of fancy of precisely that kind. I shall not concern myself with his interpretation of the ordinary, pre-theoretical belief that objects continue to exist unperceived, though he certainly exaggerates its blindness to theoretical issues. Nor shall I examine his Cartesian assumption that the causes of our sensory impressions can only be inferred. The point for which I shall argue is that his theory ought to have provided some basis for the distinction between sensible and foolish fallible inferences, and that, if it had done so, it would have been clearer whether it justified any of them, and so whether it avoided scepticism.

I am not going to pursue the question whether Hume's naturalistic system is sceptical in outcome. I am using it only as an introduction to my subject, which is the naturalism itself. But I shall not disguise my conviction that an adequate account of the origin of a belief can no more fail to contribute to its justification than an adequate account of the origin of a concept can fail to make a similar contribution.

The naturalism of Hume's account of the understanding goes deeper in the *Treatise* than in his later writings. In the *Treatise* he not only describes our habits of thought but also tries to deduce them from a single theory in the manner of Newton. The theory deals with what he calls 'natural relations between ideas',[1] and most of it is based on psychological observation. But the theory also contains two axioms which are not based on psychological observation, though he sometimes writes as if that were their basis: '*All our ideas are derived from impressions*',[2] and '*All our distinct perceptions are distinct existences*'.[3] In his later work his naturalism lacks this depth, because he gradually abandons his elaborate psychology and describes our habits of thought without trying to fit them into a single explanatory framework. Apparently, he was dissatisfied with the foundations laid in *Book I*, but did not see how to improve them and wanted to complete the edifice.

It does not follow that his later account of the understanding is shallow. Certainly, it lacks theoretical depth, but there are other ways in which naturalism can achieve profundity, and Wittgenstein may have been right in thinking that theoretical depth is for scientists rather than philosophers. Anyway, Hume's later naturalism is more informal, but it is the result of penetrating observation of our habits of thought, and it subjects them to a profound critique based on the two axioms, which, of course, he never abandoned. But his early naturalism is systematic, and that is what gives it its depth and interest.

The early psychological theory is divided into three parts. First, there is a very economical account of the contents of the mind: it contains only impressions and ideas that are derived from them and copy them. The second part is the deceptively simple thesis that belief is a vivacious idea. Then the origin of belief is described in the third and most complicated part of the theory, which analyses natural relations between ideas.

I shall concentrate on the second and third parts of this theory, because I am going to inquire whether it provides an adequate explanation of our beliefs about causation, perceived objects, and persons. But it must not be forgotten that the first part contains Hume's theory of meaning. That theory is expressed in an axiom that is not really based on psychological observation. For though the precise ways in which ideas can be derived from impressions may be discernible by personal

---

[1] *Treatise* I. i. v.   [2] Ibid. I. i. i.
[3] Ibid. I. i. vii, and Appendix.

reflection on their history, the thesis that in one way or another all ideas must be derived from impressions has to achieve some kind of fit with the distinction between genuine and spurious ideas that was already established and current. Nor must it be forgotten that his system relies at many points on the other axiom, that all our distinct perceptions are distinct existences. This axiom too needs to be supported by something more than direct psychological observation. For it is not the case that Hume tried but failed to discover real connections between distinct perceptions. On the contrary, he began by choosing discrete elements for his theory, and that is the kind of choice that would be vindicated not by his failure to discover elements of any other type, but rather by some kind of global fit between the resulting theory and human thought. These two axioms are permanent features of his philosophy, and his naturalism would have been lame without them.

At first sight, the support received by the thesis that belief is a vivacious idea appears to be purely local. Hume simply tries to report the result of direct observation of the psychological phenomenon in his own case. But he does not find it easy to formulate the result in a satisfactory way, and he vacillates between two versions of it. Sometimes he speaks of *lively colours* and *brightness*, but at other times he prefers *force, firmness*, and *steadiness*. In the end he confesses that 'it is impossible to explain perfectly this feeling or manner of conception',[1] and he characterizes it as 'that je-ne-sçai-quoi, of which it is impossible to give any definition or description, but which everyone sufficiently understands'.[2]

It is fairly clear what his difficulty was. His ideas are images, and, if the belief that a certain kind of impression is about to occur consists in an idea, the idea will need two entirely different properties. In order to carry the content of the proposition that is believed, it must possess an intrinsic property that matches the identificatory property of the expected impression. This requirement is most easily understood in a visual case, because the intrinsic property of the idea may then be a pictorial property of an image. The other property needed by the idea is an extrinsic one which will mark off belief from other propositional attitudes. Now Hume is almost aware that in a visual case the property that marks off belief must not be pictorial, because, if it were pictorial, the propositional content would change

[1] Ibid. I. 3. vii.   [2] Ibid. I. 3. viii.

as mere consideration turned into suspicion and finally into belief.[1] So it is fairer to discount his tendency to treat the mark of belief as a pictorial property of the idea, and to take his settled view to be that it is a non-pictorial property, or, more generally, an extrinsic property.

However, that is not the end of his difficulty. For when he has decided that the mark of belief must be an extrinsic property of the idea, he still has to identify the right extrinsic property, and that proves to be a difficult task because all the likely candidates seem to occur not only in cases of belief, but also in cases in which belief is not, and sometimes cannot be, involved. For example, it is obvious that an obsessive fantasy may force itself upon the mind and may haunt it steadily and even with firmness. The reason why all Hume's suggestions founder on such counter-examples is that it is impossible to develop a theory of belief that makes so little use of assertion and truth. Force and steadiness are marks of belief only in the context of a question. An image that forces itself upon the mind and maintains itself there as the pictorial answer to a definite question does amount to a belief. But the theory collapses when this context is omitted, and an analysis of the context would have to be based on the concepts of assertion and truth. So it was an illusion to suppose that a theory of belief could be supported by the kind of local evidence that Hume produces.

The theory of natural relations is intended to explain the origin of our problematical beliefs. A natural relation between two mental elements (i.e. impressions or ideas) is one that usually but not invariably sets up an association between them.[2] A problematical belief is an idea that acquires its vivacity through an association with a present impression.[3] Memory is not a problematical case, because its beliefs are ideas whose vivacity is not acquired by any detectable mental process, but by some neural process with which Hume is not concerned.[4] Perception is not problematical so long as its judgements are confined to present impressions, because the conviction produced by them is too strong to count as belief.[5] But beliefs about objects that continue to exist unperceived are problematical. So too are beliefs about persons and causal processes.

In Hume's theory there are two different ways in which relations may hold between mental elements. They may relate

[1] Ibid. I. 3. vii.   [2] Ibid. I. 3. iv–vi.
[3] Ibid. I. 3. viii.   [4] Ibid. I. 3. v.
[5] Ibid. I. 4. ii.

them through their contents, or independently of their contents. If two ideas are related through their contents, the same relation may, and sometimes will, hold between any similar pair of impressions. He regards it as a speculative question whether the relation also holds between any pair of objects that continue to exist unperceived. But the match between the related pair of ideas and similar pairs of related impressions provides him with a workable, but rudimentary theory of truth.

Every relation has an intrinsic nature, and, when we consider its intrinsic nature, Hume says that we are taking it as a philosophical relation, because philosophers extend the class of relations beyond the limit that strikes ordinary people as natural.[1] But some philosophical relations are also natural relations, because they lie within the limit that is recognized by ordinary people, and so they tend to produce associations between the mental elements that they relate.[2] He places only three relations in this sub-class: resemblance, contiguity, and causation.[3] The psychological theory of the *Treatise* is deduced from the proposition that these three relations are distinguished from other philosophical relations by the fact that they are also natural relations, and so set up the associations that produce our problematical beliefs.

The first step towards understanding the theory is to see why certain ordinary beliefs are problematical and need it to explain them. This question may be approached through Hume's classification of philosophical relations. When he considers relations strictly from the point of view of their intrinsic natures, he divides them into two classes. In the first class the relation holds necessarily between two ideas given their contents, and yields knowledge rather than belief. Resemblance and certain mathematical and logical relations belong to this class.[4] In such cases he allows the rationalist inference from ideas to things, even if the things are only interpreted phenomenally as impressions, and this gives him a theory of necessary truth. In the second class the relation still holds between the two ideas through their contents, but it only holds contingently, so that it is an open question whether it also holds between impressions. How can such contingent truths be established?

Hume does not give the same answer for all the relations in this second class, but subdivides it for this purpose. One sub-division contains contiguity while the other contains causality.

---

[1] Ibid. I. 1. v.   [2] Ibid. I. 1. iv.
[3] Ibid. I. 1. iv and 3. v.   [4] Ibid. I. 3. i.

Contiguity may be established by direct observation,[1] but causation cannot be established in this way.[2] Causal beliefs are, therefore, problematical. He could have given the same explanation of the problematical character of beliefs about persons and unperceived objects. He need not have treated identity as a relation, because he could have used two substitutes for it which would have made his theory much clearer—the co-personality of mental elements, and the co-objectuality of impressions of sensation. Like causation, these two relations evidently do not hold necessarily between mental elements, nor can their holding be established by any special impression.

It may seem surprising that Hume should put so much emphasis on the fact that resemblance, contiguity, and causation are natural relations as well as philosophical relations. For in non-problematical cases it hardly seems necessary to mention this duality of aspect. The resemblance between two ideas identified through their contents is established *a priori*, and though it may set up an association between them, the association evidently cannot play any part in producing the knowledge that they resemble one another, because it is the later effect of that knowledge. Similarly, contiguity is established by direct observation, and, if it sets up an association, it will be one that is subsequent to the formation of the conviction that the two mental elements are contiguous, and cannot, therefore produce it.

But in problematical cases, like causation, the duality of aspect of the three relations is essential to Hume's psychological theory. For when the belief that a relation holds between two impressions cannot be established either as a necessary truth or as a contingent truth based on a third, special impression, he has to explain, not only which features of the original impressions lead us to believe that the relation does hold between them, but also how they produce this belief. The first of these two explanations is provided by the analysis of the relation in its philosophical aspect, which will give the total legitimate content of the idea, or, to express this in another way, all that there can be in reality. The second explanation is provided by the analysis of the relation in its natural aspect. For this will show how the features of the original impressions produce the associations required for the belief.

So Hume's psychological theory is designed to explain the origin of problematical beliefs. But it also contains an account of

[1] Ibid. I. 2. iii.   [2] Ibid. I. 3. xiv.

the way in which such beliefs achieve the match with impressions that counts as truth in his system. They do not achieve it *a priori*, as rationalists suppose, nor by a direct adjustment to a special experience, as naïve empiricists suppose, but in a third, more complicated way, which he explains most successfully in the case of causation.

He defines causation both as a philosophical and as a natural relation. From the philosophical point of view a cause is 'an object precedent and contiguous to another, and where all the objects resembling the former are placed in like relations of priority and contiguity to those objects that resemble the latter'.[1] If he had been more cautious, he would have set up this definition on a phenomenal basis, substituting impressions for objects. Either way, the total legitimate content of the idea of causation is constant conjunction between resembling pairs of things, in each of which one member is contiguous with and prior to the other.

From the natural point of view, a cause is 'an object precedent and contiguous to another, and so united with it that the idea of the one determines the mind to form the idea of the other, and the impression of the one to form a more lively idea of the other'.[2] He is sometimes criticized on the ground that these two definitions are not necessarily equivalent, because the second, unlike the first, requires the presence and operation of a mind. But it is clear that the consecutive clause after the words 'so united with it' merely specifies the type of union through its tendency to generate in any mind that may observe it an association of two mental elements, which, on some later occasion will produce the causal belief that something resembling the second element is about to occur.

I shall not discuss the question whether this analysis of causal belief trims it too ruthlessly to fit an excessively restrictive theory of meaning. If it is not too reductive, Hume's account of the internal impression of necessitated transition certainly gives an ingenious explanation of the illegitimate element in the popular concept of causation. But my concern is with the naturalistic theory of belief, which is designed to explain how causation, when it relates a sequence of pairs of impressions, produces a reflection of itself in the mind of the observer. The reflection is a disposition to produce a vivacious idea of the second member of the pair in response to an impression re-

---

[1] Ibid., loc. cit.   [2] Ibid., loc. cit.

sembling the first one. It is, therefore, a causal disposition, and it is caused by the original observed causation functioning as a natural relation.

Hume's analysis of causation, considered as a philosophical relation, is plausible, and his account of the way in which it functions as a natural relation producing a mental reflection of itself is ingenious, and the whole treatment offers a promising way of avoiding the choice between rationalism and naïve empiricism. But the explanation of the origin of causal belief was designed to fit into a general theory, which would also serve to explain other problematical beliefs, and Hume is less successful in carrying out this more ambitious project.

The general theory is that belief is an idea endowed with vivacity through its association with a present impression, and that such associations are produced by the three natural relations, resemblance, contiguity, and causation. When this theory is applied to the analysis of causation itself, it seems at first sight to fit. For observed causation, functioning as a natural relation, produces an association which, in its turn, produces a vivacious idea in response to a present impression. But when observed causation is analysed as a philosophical relation, it turns out that its most important ingredient is constant con-junction. It is true that contiguity is another ingredient, but it is a less important natural relation between the members of each pair in the sequence, and resemblance between the mem-bers of each pair is not needed at all. Of course, the first members in each pair must resemble each other, and so too must the second members. But that is a different requirement, because, though this resemblance, like any other, may be re-garded as a natural relation, it certainly does not function as such in this case. For it does not set up the association, but only determines the two sets of members which are going to be associated by some other means, viz. by constant conjunction and contiguity.

So there is some confusion in Hume's general theory about the origins of belief. The theory is that resemblance, contiguity, and causation are three equipollent natural relations, each capable of setting up an association that will produce a belief. But in the case of causation it is constant conjunction that does most of the work of setting up the association, and causation is the only one of the three natural relations that involves constant conjunction. Contiguity has a minor role, but it does at least relate the members of each pair in the sequence, while resemblance does not even do that. It is true that all three natural relations are involved in causal inference, but their contributions are neither equal nor of the same kind. They could not be equal, because causation includes the other two and adds to them something much more weighty as evidence—constant conjunction, and resemblance does not even make a contribution of the right kind. For when a natural relation sets up an association of ideas that produces a belief, it is essential that it should hold between the two things that the ideas match. But in the case of causal inference resemblance does not meet this requirement. Later I shall analyse another, more important case of failure to meet this requirement—a failure that occurs in Hume's account of the ordinary belief that objects continue to exist unperceived.

The confusion in his general theory of the origins of belief is more evident when resemblance and contiguity are taken on their own, apart from causation. For then the weakness of these two natural relations is immediately exposed. The observed contiguity of two things is not enough to support the belief that the next time one of them is found the other will still be found beside it. A general proposition is evidently needed, and it is unlikely to be the proposition that nothing moves. Whatever it is, it will need to be based on some constant conjunction. So contiguity alone is a completely powerless natural relation.

Resemblance is in a worse plight, because it is not even clear what the belief would be in a case in which resemblance was operating alone. If a present impression produces an idea associated with it by resemblance, the idea needs a reference in order to function as a belief. But Hume's theory of belief omits all propositional details, and in this kind of case it is not clear what material could be used to supplement the theory and give the belief a definite reference. On some occasions the belief would be that the next impression of sensation will resemble the present one, and in his account of the ordinary belief in unperceived objects Hume attaches great weight to this kind of constancy. But this belief too needs a general proposition, more subtle than the proposition that nothing changes, and based on some constant conjunction. Incidentally, this kind of inference ought to have led him to add something to his thesis that resemblance holds necessarily between two mental elements given their contents. He should have added that, when a mental element is specified not by its content but by its place in a sequence, it can only be a contingent fact that it resembles a present impression.

In one way it is unfair to make these points against Hume. For he is aware that the only sensible kind of inference to a new factual conclusion is causal inference, which depends on custom generated by observed constant conjunction. So he admits that resemblance and contiguity, operating on their own, do not produce sensible beliefs, and he actually considers the objection that, if his theory were correct, they would do so.[1] But as Kemp Smith showed long ago,[2] his answer to the objection is a wholly inadequate defence of his general theory. He merely argues that resemblance between cause and effect sometimes reinforces a causal inference, and points out that a visit to the scene of some supposed historical event sometimes reinforces the belief that it actually occurred. Such observations clearly will not save the theory, and he shows a tendency to modify it in this section of the *Treatise* by saying that a present impression can give an associated idea a liveliness that does not amount to belief. But that would reopen every question.

It is not enough that he should be aware of the fact that the only sensible kind of inference to a new factual conclusion is causal inference. In the *Treatise* he is not content with recording this fact. He is trying to achieve a more systematic kind of naturalism, which will not only list the kinds of inductive inference that we find acceptable, but also relate them to a general theory. Now the general theory might not justify our grading of the evidence, but it ought to explain it, and the explanation should make some contribution towards justifying it. But Hume's general theory does not begin to do these things, because it does not provide any basis for the distinction between sensible and foolish inferences to new factual conclusions.

It is possible to see how the theory lost contact with the phenomena. Association is first introduced to account for the occurrence of ideas, and associations with this function really are produced by each of the three natural relations, resemblance, contiguity, and causation. But when association is given the altogether different function of generating belief, it can be produced only by causation or by some other relation reinforced by constant conjunction. Hume himself points out this fact, but he never revises his general theory to fit it. Perhaps he fails to see the need for revision in the *Treatise*, and perhaps the reason for this is that so much of Book I is taken up

---

[1] Ibid. I. 3. ix.   [2] '*The Philosophy of David Hume*', pp. 378–82.

with the application of the theory to causation, which is more successful because causation is the favoured exception.

Since Hume gradually abandoned his general psychological theory in his later works, it might seem appropriate to regard it as an excrescence on the *Treatise*, with no effect on his analysis of problematical beliefs. But this would be a mistake. For, as I shall now show, one of the flaws in the theory vitiates his account of the ordinary belief that objects continue to exist unperceived.

He often expresses this belief as the identity-statement, that what is perceived now is the same as what was perceived earlier. But he is not especially concerned with the criteria for reidentifying perceived objects, any more than with the criteria for reidentifying persons. His main concern is always with the principles of union, which in this case have to span an interruption of perception. Consequently, what he investigates is really a relation, co-objectuality. Now according to him, ordinary people do not distinguish between perceptions (i.e. in this case impressions of sensation) and objects.[1] So when he consults them in order to discover the category of the terms that they take to be related by co-objectuality, the result is unclear. He represents their answer as 'Perceptions'. But this answer is supposed to be given at a pre-theoretical stage, with no distinction drawn between perceptions and objects, and so the inference, 'Therefore, impressions of sensation', may be blocked by opacity. The situation would have been easier to grasp if he had represented their answer as 'What is immediately perceived', or, more briefly, 'Data'.

There is another point on which the beliefs of ordinary people need interpretation. Do they believe that data continue to exist when perception is interrupted, and that, when they are perceived, they would still have existed even if they had not been perceived? Hume credits them with affirmative answers to both questions.[2] So he does not suppose that they regard unperceived data as mere possibilities in the spirit of phenomenalism. (If they had taken that view, it would not have actually been phenomenalism, because they do not unequivocally identify data with impressions of sensation.) On this point he is on their side. For though he rejects the suggestion that data are specifically different from impressions of sensation,[3] he never considers the suggestion that, when they are not perceived, they are mere possibilities.

---

[1] *Treatise* I. 4. ii.   [2] Ibid., loc. cit.
[3] Ibid. I. 2. vi.

If ordinary people believe that the fact, that two detached
sequences of perceived data are co-objectual entails that they
actually continue to exist in the interval during which perception is interrupted, their belief is obviously problematical.
It cannot be a deliverance of reason, because it can be denied
without any change in the contents of the ideas involved in
it. It cannot be based on sensation unaided by inference,
because no impressions of sensation can possibly support
hypotheses about something that is not perceived.[1] If neither
rationalism nor naïve empiricism can account for it, the explanation must be sought in Hume's general psychological
theory of the origins of belief. Co-objectuality must be analysed
as a philosophical relation, and its analysis must include natural
relations capable of producing associations to sustain the ordinary belief in it.

Before examining Hume's attempt to carry out this task, it
is as well to state the conditions of success, taking care not to
exaggerate them. The ordinary belief does not have to be
justified rationally, but it does have to be related to evidence
in a way that is commonly accepted as sensible. When co-
objectuality is analysed as a philosophical relation, the belief
that it holds between two sets of data must be generated by
the natural relations included in its analysis, and it must be
generated in accordance with principles that we would not
reject as foolish or flighty. Of course, the belief may be trimmed
a little, in order to get a match with the available evidence,
but it must not be shorn of its essentials. Finally, the general
principles used in this particular case ought to find their place,
and ought to be given some distinguishing characterization, in
the general psychological theory.

I do not think that Hume succeeds in this task, and he does
not think so either.[2] His difficulty is clear. When two detached
sequences of perceived data are co-objectual, ordinary people
postulate unperceived data to fill the gap between them. But
he treats the predicate 'unperceived' as a scientific predicate
determining a class of data, like visual data or tactual data.[3]
Now unperceived data are related to perceived data by resemblance when it is a case of constancy, and by causation
when it is a case of coherence,[4] and if the holding of these
two relations could be established by experience, they would
function as natural relations occurring in the analysis of the

[1] Ibid. I. 4. ii.   [2] Ibid., loc. cit.
[3] Ibid., loc. cit.   [4] Ibid., loc. cit.

philosophical relation, co-objectuality, and explaining the ordinary belief in it. This is how he treats co-objectuality when perception is not interrupted,[1] and if he could treat it in the same way when perception is interrupted, he could explain the ordinary belief in it in much the same way that he explained the ordinary belief in causation. But unfortunately, in this case experience cannot establish that the two natural relations hold,[2] because some of the related terms belong to a class that is never experienced. This compels him to place the ordinary belief on a weaker basis.

His reconstruction of its foundations is elaborate. What has to be explained is our tendency to extrapolate the constancy or coherence of perceived data beyond the limits of experience. His explanation begins with an analysis of identity. Strictly speaking, he tells us, identity requires both invariance and continuity. But continuity is lacking when all that we have is two detached sequences of perceived data. In spite of this lack, we tend to attribute identity, because our experience of the two detached sequences feels very like our experience of a single continuous sequence. However, we are bothered by the fact that the attribution of identity conflicts with the strict requirement of continuity. So we have developed a second tendency which removes the conflict—the tendency to picture appropriate unperceived data filling the gap between the two perceived sequences. But these pictures, or ideas, need vivacity in order to amount to belief. The crux of the whole account is Hume's explanation of the way in which they get the required vivacity. They get it from the present impressions of sensation belonging to the second sequence, and the present impressions of memory derived from the first sequence. (He often speaks of impressions rather than of ideas of memory.) The relation that transfers the vivacity from these impressions to the ideas of unperceived data is causation. For the impressions cause both the tendency to attribute identity and the tendency to picture unperceived data in order to remove the resulting contradiction.[3]

If this is how ordinary people come to believe in the existence of unperceived data, their inference is a foolish one. For the causation that functions as a natural relation producing their belief does not relate two sets of observed data as it did in the previous case, the case of the problematical belief in causation itself. What it relates in this case is a set of observed data and

---

[1] Ibid. I. 1. vi.   [2] Ibid. I. 4. ii.
[3] Ibid., loc. cit.

two mental tendencies. It is obvious that any inference drawn on this principle is altogether flighty.

It is questionable whether Hume's general theory really allows such an inference. As I stated it, the theory requires all operative natural relations to hold between perceived data. This requirement must be met if the idea that some relations have two aspects is going to open up a way out of the dilemma between rationalism and naïve empiricism. That door remains open only so long as the situation can be schematized in the following way: the problematical philosophical relation must be analysed into relations between impressions of sensation, some of which will function as natural relations producing the belief that the philosophical relation really does hold between the impressions of sensation.

This schema amounts to a theory of truth for problematical beliefs. The ideas that make up the belief must form a pattern that matches the pattern of the impressions of sensation. Sometimes, as in the case of causation, it is only mismatch that can be firmly established, and sometimes the pattern of ideas must be trimmed of certain excesses before there can be any hope of a match. But there is one feature of the schema that can never be compromised: any natural relation that serves to produce the association supporting the belief must belong to the reality that is matched, even if it also appears on the signifying side, which bears the onus of matching. The case of causation illustrates this requirement. In that case causation itself, analysed into contiguity, priority, and constant conjunction, relates the original impressions of sensation and that is the essential base of its operations. It then causes on the signifying side an association of ideas, like any other natural relation, and the association itself operates as a causal disposition. But whatever causation does to ideas, it must begin by relating the original impressions of sensation. This condition is violated by Hume's account of the ordinary belief in the continued existence of unperceived objects.

However, when he sets out his general theory, he does not explicitly state this requirement. So it is possible to take the error to lie in the theory itself, rather than in its application to this particular case. Either way, the result is a failure to discriminate between sensible and foolish principles of nondeductive inference.

Hume himself is dissatisfied with his account of the origin of this particular problematical belief, partly because the mechanism of the inference is so weak. He says, 'I cannot conceive how such trivial qualities of the fancy, conducted by such false suppositions, can ever lead to any solid and rational system.'[1] But he does not locate the central weakness, which is the misplacing of the operative natural relation. He also has another reason for dissatisfaction. He equates the data of ordinary people with impressions of sensation, and he argues that, though it is conceivable that impressions of sensation may exist in isolation, experiment shows that in fact they depend on our organs of sense.[2] So this particular problematical belief is actually false, and it is to nature's credit that it succeeds in forcing it on us.

I shall not examine Hume's interpretation of the data of ordinary people, or explore other ways out of the impasse into which it leads him. Nor have I time for his brilliant critique of his predecessors' theories of perception. My only point about this section of the *Treatise* is that in it the general theory of the origin of belief is applied in a way that ruins it.

In the Appendix to the *Treatise* Hume does not mention his dissatisfaction with his treatment of the ordinary belief in the continued existence of unperceived objects, perhaps because he assumes that his system could rest on phenomenal foundations. But he does say that his treatment of the third problematical case, personal identity, was mistaken, and that he does not know how to put it right. Since he analyses co-personality in the same way as co-objectuality, it is an interesting question why he is not dissatisfied with the *Treatise* on both scores.

I shall now try to show that he gives the wrong reason for rejecting his earlier account of co-personality. The reason that he gives is that his general theory fails to explain the ordinary belief in co-personality, because it appeals to natural relations that do not support it adequately—more or less the complaint that I have been making against his account of co-objectuality. But the true reason, I shall argue, is something else.

In the text of the *Treatise* co-personality is explicitly modelled on co-objectuality.[3] It is represented as a philosophical relation that holds between pairs of mental elements. But it does not hold necessarily between the ideas of any two mental elements, given the contents of those ideas, nor is it based on any special impression. So Hume analyses it, hoping to find that its total legitimate content will include enough natural relations to

[1] Ibid., loc. cit.   [2] Ibid., loc. cit.
[3] Ibid. I. 4. vi.

explain our belief that it holds. The two natural relations that he turns up are resemblance and causation. Causation produces what he called 'coherence' in his treatment of co-objectuality, but he takes resemblance to produce recurrences in this case, rather than constancies, illustrating it with the example of images of memory. The function of resemblance and causation is to generate associations between the ideas of pairs of mental elements, and so to produce the beliefs that the original elements in the pairs are co-personal.

There is in this case the same difficulty that there was in the case of co-objectuality: he thinks that, strictly speaking, identity is incompatible with change of composition and with interruption, both of which are common in any mental history. Nevertheless, causation and resemblance make the transition from the first member of a related pair to the second member feel like a transition without interruption, and resemblance makes it feel like one without change, and so we are seduced into picturing the mind as a continuing entity. In order to complete his explanation, he has to say what gives such pictures the vivacity required for belief. The main difference between his account of co-personality and his account of co-objectuality is that he is inexplicit on this last point.

This is understandable. For the required vivacity has to be derived from an impression of memory of the earlier element in the pair and from the later element, which, we may assume, is now present to the mind. But the latter may happen to be an idea, in which case, according to Hume's theory, it will not be a source of vivacity. However, it is obvious that in fact a present idea is as good a source of vivacity *for this particular belief* as a present impression. The explanation of this fact is that it is sufficient in this case that there should be consciousness of the idea, as, according to him, there always is. But the theory of vivacity would have to be rewritten to accommodate this point, and that is why he says so little about the source of the vivacity required for the belief in co-personality.

Hume's own reason for his dissatisfaction with his analysis of co-personality and with his account of the origin of the ordinary belief in it is interesting but incomplete. As usual, the account avoids both rationalism and naïve empiricism and relies on a sophisticated criterion of match and on a certain amount of trimming of the ordinary belief in order to achieve it. In the Appendix he is still convinced that this solution is on the right lines, but he says, 'I find myself involved in such a labyrinth that, I must confess, I neither know how to correct my former opinions, nor how to render them consistent.'[1] His difficulty is that he is unable to 'explain the principles that unite our successive perceptions in our thought or consciousness'.[2] He has analysed co-personality as a philosophical relation, but he now finds that the two natural relations occurring in its analysis, resemblance and causation, are insufficient to explain the ordinary belief in it. He evidently supposes that there is a short-coming in the detailed development of his theory, a shortcoming that is shown up when it is applied to the ordinary belief in co-personality, and he is not envisaging the possibility that this belief could not be explained by any variant of his theory.

This is somewhat obscured by his observation that there was some inconsistency in his earlier account of co-personality, especially when he tries to explain what the inconsistency was. 'In short, there are two principles which I cannot render consistent, nor is it in my power to renounce either of them, *viz. that all our distinct perceptions are distinct existences*, and *that the mind never perceives any real connection among distinct existences*. Did our perceptions either inhere in something simple and individual, or did the mind perceive some real connection among them, there would be no difficulty in the case.'[3]

It sounds as if he means that the two principles are inconsistent with one another. But he cannot mean anything so absurd. He must mean that the two principles prevent him from adopting a rationalist account of co-personality, and so, since it is equally impossible for him to adopt a naïve empiricist account, he is forced to look for an adequate explanation along the lines of his own sophisticated empiricism. He must find such an explanation, if he is going to compose all the elements— including the essential features of the ordinary belief—into a coherent picture. But, he is saying, he cannot fit all the pieces together, because his philosophy does not allow him to include all the essentials of the ordinary belief. In short, the two principles pose the problem and he is unable to find a solution in which everything falls into place, and the discrepancy between the available evidence and the actual belief is too great to be removed by any trimming of the belief.

However, he does not tell us precisely what is wrong with the explanation offered in the *Treatise*, and he only expresses his

---

[1] Appendix to the *Treatise*.   [2] Ibid., loc. cit.
[3] Ibid., loc. cit.

conviction that it ought to be possible to find a successful explanation along those lines. I think that the reason why he has no more to say is that he has not succeeded in diagnosing his own earlier error. He believes that what is needed is an improved account of the principles of union that will subsume this difficult case under his general psychological theory. But the truth is that no such account can be given of co-personality.

Since this is a familiar truth today, I shall not dwell on all the details, but I shall end this lecture with a brief demonstration of their impact on Hume's theory.

His diagnosis of his former error is that resemblance and causation do not really explain the union between co-personal mental elements, and that they need to be reinforced by stronger links. But this cannot be right, because such elements do not need to be related in any way through their contents in order to be co-personal. It is true that a sequence that exhibited no such patterns would be a disintegrated mind, but the elements in it would still be co-personal. Of course, the concept of a person would apply to such a case in an attenuated form, because the so-called person would have no sense of his own identity. But such deficiencies do not exclude co-personality.

Hume writes as if he starts with a class of elements directly accessible to himself through present experience or experience-memory, and then has to find a suitably related sub-class, just as he had to find suitably related sub-classes in the other two cases, causation and co-objectuality. But this cannot be right, because in fact nobody has direct memory-like access to others' elements as well as to his own, and so nobody is faced with the question, which directly accessible elements are related to the present moment in his mental history in ways that make them his. Of course, we can imagine the human species endowed with quasi-memory as well as with memory.[1] But Hume is certainly not doing this, but trying to develop a theory on the basis of our present endowments.

When he laments the lack of real connection between co-personal elements, he is overlooking the important fact that one of his could not have been anyone else's. But this fact is not the result of the contents of elements, but, rather, of the sequences in which each happens to begin to exist, whatever its content. To adapt his metaphor, it is not only the actors' parts that begin to exist on stage, but also the actors themselves.

[1] See S. Shoemaker, 'Persons and their Pasts', *American Journal of Philosophy*, 1970.

Then ought he to have paid more attention to the relations that hold between elements independently of their contents? Certainly, that would be necessary in order to allow for the disorderly contents of a disintegrated mind. But it would not have provided him with another way of showing that his elements are necessarily his. For causal relations between elements that have nothing to do with their contents hold contingently, like any other causal relations, and so cannot be established in the rationalist way, through the contents of the ideas of the related elements. However, if he had investigated those relations that hold between elements contingently and independently of their contents, and if he had set on one side the trivial necessary truth about ownership, he might have called off the search for stronger content-based links. At least, it is clear that its motivation is a mistaken diagnosis of his earlier error.

So the final verdict must be an ironical one. Hume's general psychological theory gives a faulty account of fallible inferences and of the origins of the associations that support them. He himself makes this criticism, but mainly of the application of the theory to co-personality. Yet in that particular case the real trouble is something else.

Throughout this lecture, I have used Hume's terminology, modernizing it as little as possible. In particular, I have expressed his theories in terms of his own distinction between philosophical and natural relations. Because his theory is pluralistic and atomistic, his difficulties are best presented as he presents them, as difficulties about relations. His idea, that some relations have two aspects is the key to the sophisticated theory of match that he develops when he is analysing and explaining our problematical beliefs. Through it we can understand both why the theory fails, and why he thinks that it fails. But it is a noble failure and there is more philosophy in it than in many more successful enterprises.

ABSOLUTE IDEALISM

By A. M. QUINTON

I

PHILOSOPHICAL movements lead two different lives. On the one hand a body of ideas is formulated, published, accepted, and finally superseded; on the other, at the institutional level, leading positions in the academic system are occupied by the exponents of the movement's ideas. Naturally these two careers are not coincident in time. New ideas are normally produced by unimportant people; the holders of important posts disseminate the ideas they acquired in their comparatively unimportant youth. As a result the dating of a philosophical movement is a slightly complicated business.

Considered as a purely intellectual phenomenon the interesting episode of absolute idealism in British philosophy can be dated with a fair degree of precision. The first seriously professional publications in which this point of view is to be found came out in 1874. That was the year of T. H. Green's long and arduously destructive critical introduction to his and Grose's edition of Hume's *Treatise of Human Nature*, of F. H. Bradley's first essay *The Presuppositions of Critical History*, of William Wallace's translation of Hegel's smaller logic (viz. Book I of the *Enzyklopädie*), and also of the beginning of the translation of Lotze's *System of Philosophy* by a group of distinguished British idealists. Two years later the first classic of the school came out: Bradley's *Ethical Studies*, the most explicitly Hegelian of his works.

Green was the acknowledged leader of the school and in many ways its most compelling personality. Beside his career of active responsibility in education and in public life that of Bradley looks pretentious and self-indulgent. Outside the field of technical philosophy narrowly conceived, Green was certainly the most influential of the idealists. He died in 1882 soon after the school was established. The year after, a group of his admirers brought out *Essays in Philosophical Criticism*, in which his more or less Hegelian methods were applied over a broad range of subjects, and his own chief work *Prolegomena to Ethics* was published, as were also the first edition of Bradley's *Principles of Logic* and Caird's short but substantial book on Hegel.

Green's death deprived the school of a prime unifying factor, but its intellectual dominance continued for the next twenty years. Seth, five years after editing the memorial volume to Green, sounded the first note of protest against the dissolution of the theist's God and of the free and immortal human soul in the all-engulfing Hegelian Absolute in his *Hegelianism and Personality*. This introduced a style of opposition to idealist orthodoxy that was to culminate in the system of McTaggart. On the way it made a detour through pragmatism, which never amounted to anything very much in this country, for all the polemical energies and copious productiveness of F. C. S. Schiller. At Oxford Cook Wilson carried on a somewhat furtive resistance to the reigning opinions from the end of the century (his lectures, *Statement and Inference*, were not published until 1926, eleven years after his death). At Cambridge Sidgwick represented an older way of thinking, but Sorley was an adherent and so, more brilliantly and heretically, was McTaggart.

The first really fundamental assault on idealism did not come until 1903, the year of Russell's *Principles of Mathematics* and Moore's *Refutation of Idealism*. Russell and Moore initiated a wholly opposed style of thought. Its uninterrupted development and augmentation of strength make it reasonable to date the end of idealism's full intellectual dominance from that year, just a decade after the idealist movement's most imposing expression in Bradley's *Appearance and Reality*.

But idealist professors continued to head university philosophy departments for a considerable time after 1903. In Oxford J. A. Smith and Collingwood occupied the chair of metaphysics in succession from 1910 to 1941. In Cambridge, although Moore was appointed to a chair in 1925, the year of McTaggart's death, Sorley remained professor of moral philosophy until 1933. In other universities the idealist hegemony was more enduring and persisted in Scotland until very recent years. Until well into the 1920s idealists held nearly all the leading positions in the philosophy departments of British universities and continued to be the largest group in the philosophical professoriate until 1945. Nothing shows the intellectually anachronistic character of this state of affairs more poignantly than the very high level of technological unemployment of idealists within the philosophical profession. A remarkable number of them nimbly overcame this misfortune by becoming vice-chancellors. The Hegelian mode of thought, with its combination of practical realism and theoretical nebulosity, is a remarkably serviceable instrument for the holders of high administrative positions.

Absolute idealism, then, exercised its full intellectual authority in Britain in the three decades between 1874 and 1903. I shall try to explain the rapidity with which it secured its hold to the absence of any very compelling alternative, to the fact that it arose in something very like a philosophical vacuum. For the two decades after 1903 it remained the best entrenched movement institutionally and it still constituted a considerable intellectual force. But after the deaths of Bradley and McTaggart, in 1924 and 1925, and Moore's appointment to a chair in Cambridge in the latter year, no new idealist works of any significance appeared in Britain except those of Collingwood. Twenty years later still its institutional hold was finally lost.

This episode in the history of British philosophy raises a number of interesting questions. The first I shall attempt to answer is that of why it began when it did and, arising out of that, how idealism managed to establish itself so rapidly. This leads on to the problem posed by the very late according of serious attention to Hegel and to the connected problem of the extent of absolute idealism's dependence on him. I shall defend the conventional view that British idealism is, more than anything else, Hegelian in inspiration. I shall end with a brief presentation of the main theses of absolute idealism as systematically dependent on the principle of internal relations, which is itself an ontological expression of the nature of the distinction between reason and understanding as it was conceived by Hegel.

II

First, then, why did absolute idealism emerge in Britain when it did, two-thirds of the way through the nineteenth century, around the time of Stirling's *Secret of Hegel* (1865) and the beginning of Green's career as a philosophical teacher? Perhaps the most substantial reason is that it met two ideological needs that were being felt with a particular intensity. The first of these was for a defence of the Christian religion sufficiently respectable to confront the ever more formidable scientific influences that were working to undermine religious belief. The second was the need for a politics of social responsibility to set against triumphant *laissez-faire*, of political altruism to counter the idea that un-inhibited competition between self-interested individuals was the indispensable engine of human progress.

The religious scepticism of the Enlightenment had been directed more against the particular details of Christianity than the fundamentals of religious belief of any kind. Deism was a more common position than atheism; Voltaire, with his belief in a Newtonian regulator of the order of nature, is a more typical figure than Hume, with his altogether more radical assault, both philosophical and historical, on all forms of religion. The Incarnation, the literal inspiration of the Bible, the mysteries of the Sacraments and the Apostolic Succession were the targets— not the existence of God. Furthermore, general arguments against religion like Hume's did not depend on any special knowledge for their force, only on a combination of acuteness and courage.

In the nineteenth century, however, autonomous develop-ments in science, undertaken with no thought of their bearing on religion, exerted a dissolving influence upon it in a way that Newtonian physics had not. Geology, for example, by discarding the orthodox conception of the age of the world, supplied a counter-religious account of the nature of the universe in time parallel to that supplied by Copernicus about its nature in space. This, however, was more a difficulty for Christianity, as cur-rently conceived, than for religion in general. The same is true of historical scholarship about the Bible, as exhibited in such works as Strauss's *Leben Jesu*. There is, indeed, no real irony in the fact that the British defenders of religion in the late nineteenth century should have gone for help to the Hegel who, earlier in the century, had inspired the biblical criticism which had contributed to the need for a defence. Hegel may have been, in a broad sense, a religious philosopher in view of his insistence on the essentially spiritual nature of the world. But the Christian-ity he was prepared to endorse, however laudatory the terms in which he spoke of it, as for instance, the 'absolute religion', was remote from the literalism of prevailing religious orthodoxy. His ideas about religion involved a massive disencumbrance of faith from rationally indigestible elements, which were demoted by him to the status of figurative representations of metaphysical truth.

The scientific development that collided with religion in general, rather than orthodox Christianity in particular, was, of course, the evolutionary biology of Darwin. His theory of the

emergence of man on the earth, as the result of competitive
selection from random variations thrown up among more
primitive animal species, struck at the foundations of religion as
a whole in two ways. In the first place it disqualified the largest
and most emotionally important range of evidence that existed
for the argument from design. The gratifying adaptedness of
man to the natural world in which he finds himself was now
revealed as the outcome, explicable on mechanical principles,
of a vast sequence of minute accidents. It no longer demanded
to be understood as fulfilling the purpose of an infinite and
benevolent intelligence. The argument from design was thus
enfeebled, not, as at the hands of Hume, in its more or less
elusive logic, but, with much more devastating effect, in its
factual premisses.

Secondly, Darwinism seemed to refute the dualistic conception of man as a compound of immortal soul and perishable
body, of divine reason and animal passion. Dualism of this kind
is a central feature of all the higher religions. It had also been a
cardinal principle of the great tradition of European philosophers from Plato and St. Augustine to Kant. The idea that
man is a material constituent of the natural order, whose
distinguishing peculiarities are susceptible of the same kind of
mechanical explanation as those of ordinary natural objects,
had been confined hitherto to more or less scandalous specula-
tors like Hobbes. The members of the associationist tradition
that derived from him had often been enthusiastically religious,
for example, Hartley. If the utilitarians proper, in whom this
tradition culminated, had hardly been devout, the last and
greatest of them, John Stuart Mill, had allowed in his late essay
on theism that the hypothesis of a limited God had a fair measure
of probability and he had insisted both on the radical distinctness of mind and body and on the irreducibility of the mind to
its component experiences. But with Darwin the conception
of man as wholly a part of nature acquired a kind of solid factual
support that it had never had before, and which had been only
faintly anticipated by Harvey's discovery of the circulation of
the blood. Darwin did not, of course, strictly prove that man is a
natural object, like, if more complex than, any other. The
implication could be circumvented by regarding the evolutionary development that Darwin described as the instrument
by which God created an earthly vehicle for the immortal soul.
But the immediate impact of Darwin's views, supposing them to
be true, seemed fatal to the religious view of man and the world.

Darwin's most brilliant expositor, T. H. Huxley, began his career of elaborating the wider implications of Darwinism with *Man's Place in Nature* in 1863, the year of Lyell's geological demonstration of the errors of orthodoxy about the antiquity of mankind. In 1871 Darwin's own *Descent of Man* was published, explicitly extending his principles to the human species. Thus, Stirling's *Secret of Hegel* in 1865 and the group of more professional Hegelian writings in 1874 were very timely, if help for religion was to be looked for in that direction.

Indeed, as a means for the defence of religion, the philosophy of Hegel had two great merits. First, Hegel succeeded in steering religion clear of a head-on collision with science by jettisoning the more factually concrete details of Christianity and by reinterpreting those elements of the faith to which the new scientific developments were most destructive as poetic images of the abstract metaphysical principle of the spirituality of the world. Darwin was fatal to a literal reading of the story of Adam and Eve, but not to the Hegelian reinterpretation of that story as a metaphor for the emergence of man on earth as a crucial point in the self-externalization of the Absolute Mind.

Secondly, Hegel was himself, in a very large sense of the word, an evolutionist. The dialectical process could be and was understood as setting out the stages of the development of forms of existence in time, though as a matter of rational necessity not cumulative accident. Admittedly, in the little read and regarded part of his work that contains his philosophy of nature, Hegel rejected biological evolution. 'It has been an inept conception of earlier and later "*Naturphilosophie*"', he wrote (*Encyclopedia*, sec. 249), 'to regard the progression and transition of one natural form and sphere into a higher as an outwardly actual production. . . . Thinking consideration must deny itself such nebulous, at bottom, sensuous, conceptions as . . . the origin of the more highly developed animal organizations from the lower.' Nevertheless, the dialectical process is a matter of the emergence of higher entities out of a conflict between their less-developed anticipations. If Hegel denies its application in a temporal sense to non-human nature as much as to the pure concepts of logic, he does take it to be temporal in its application to the individual mind, in its ascent from sense-certainty to absolute knowledge, and again to human society, in its passage from the primitive tribal family to the fully rational state. It would be no great modification of Hegel's system to regard the dialectic as temporal in nature as well as in mind and society.

The Absolute Idealists themselves testify to the serviceability of their doctrines for the purposes of religious apologetic and reveal the attractions that this fact held for them. As Muirhead says, 'British idealism has been from the first a philosophy of religion' (*The Platonic Tradition*, p. 197). Stirling, the first in the field, is disarmingly explicit about it. Hegel, he wrote, 'is the greatest abstract thinker of Christianity', and again, 'the Hegelian system supports and gives effect to every claim of this religion'; Hegel's views 'conciliate themselves admirably with the revelation of the New Testament'. T. H. Green was a seriously religious man in his plain, earnest, non-sacerdotal way, an evangelical who sought rational foundations for his faith and laboriously worked them out in his conception of the 'eternal consciousness', the 'spiritual principle in man and nature' expounded in the first part of his *Prolegomena to Ethics*. In a Kantian fashion he argues that nature, as we know it, is a related and orderly system, which presupposes the ordering work of the knower's mind in its construction. But for this knowledge to be more than subjective improvisation, unintelligibly set off by a Kantian thing-in-itself, for it to be genuinely objective knowledge, an all-inclusive mind must be presupposed of which our finite minds are in some sense parts. Green affirms that 'there is one spiritual and self-conscious being of which all that is real is the activity and expression; that we are all related to this spiritual being, not merely as parts of the world which is its expression, but as partakers in some inchoate measure of the self-consciousness through which it at once constitutes itself and distinguishes itself from the world ... and that this participation is the source of morality and religion' (*Works*, vol. iii, p. 145). If this seems pantheistic, on a natural interpretation, so does Hegel. What is unquestionable is its positively religious intention.

The religious interest is even more prominent in the other, and more unreservedly Hegelian, initiator of British idealism: Edward Caird. His main constructive work, as distinct from the elaborate interpretations of the philosophy of Kant which make up the bulk of his output, are his Gifford lectures of 1893: *The Evolution of Religion*. In them God is defined as the infinite, but not Kantianly transcendent, being that is the unity that includes and fulfils all things. In his little book on Hegel Caird describes him as, and praises him for, securing 'the moral and religious basis of human existence'.

The two great later idealists, Bradley and McTaggart, were not defenders of religion in any ordinary sense and were far from being Christians. Bradley's Absolute is not a mind but a harmonious tissue of experience and in his system metaphysics transcends and surpasses religion much more radically and dismissively than it does in his more Hegelian predecessors. McTaggart, defining religion as 'an emotion resting on a conviction of a harmony between ourselves and the universe at large' (*Some Dogmas of Religion*, p. 3), accepts this conviction in a form which excludes God altogether, in however dilute a conception. For McTaggart the Absolute is a community of immortal and disembodied finite souls who are related by love. But the lesser lights of idealism, in particular Caird's pupils Jones, Muirhead, and Mackenzie, followed him in treating metaphysics as a rational fulfilment of the religious impulse.

III

The second large intellectual need that absolute idealism catered for was that for a political theory which, by taking a more exalted conception of the state than that traditional in Britain since Locke and the establishment of a parliamentary monarchy, could provide a more rational solution to the social problems of the age than unhindered economic competition was able to offer. By the mid nineteenth century the transfer of ultimate political power from the landowning class to the proprietors of industry, symbolized by the repeal of the Corn Laws, was well under way, even if it was not to be finally completed until the time of Bonar Law and Baldwin. Liberalism, at this time, was the party of the manufacturing interest. The freedom from state interference required by industrialists for their economic activities allied with them the parallel interest of dissenters in removing the disabilities imposed for the protection of the established church, an interest whose chief political effect in the later part of the century was to obstruct, complicate, and enfeeble the national system of education. The traditional instruments of government had failed to respond adequately to the major social changes of the period: the great increase in population, the rapid growth of large industrial cities, and the special problems of destitution to which the new forms of social living gave rise.

The progressive, reforming impulse has expressed itself in a fitful and irregular way in the history of British political thought. In the civil war there was an outburst of democratic radicalism of varying degrees of extremity. It seems to have gone under-

ground, even to have disappeared altogether or to have emi-
grated to the American colonies, until well on towards the end
of the eighteenth century. But, since it was at least latently active
in the developing social attitudes of the American colonists,
when it came to the surface in the American Revolution it
evoked a response in Britain from Paine, Priestley, and Price.
This type of radicalism, sympathetic to both the American and
French Revolutions, achieved its extreme theoretical expression
in Godwin's *Political Justice*, but its doubly scandalous character,
as unpatriotic in its fondness for the allied national enemies,
France and the United States, and as destructive in its attitude
to religion, ensured that its influence would be marginal. (Price
and Priestley were both devout ministers of religion, but Paine
was at best a deist while Godwin, for all his Sandemanian
beginnings, was an atheist.)

Thus in the early nineteenth century the only effective reforming tendency in British political thought was the philosophical,
rather than democratic, radicalism of Bentham and his followers. In its early phases the utilitarian movement was concerned
with the mainly negative task of legal and political reform.
This task was negative because seen as one of clearing away the
complex and irrational encumbrance of ancient laws and
institutions behind which 'sinister interests' lurked and profited.
Freed from these obstructions, men, it was expected, would
improve themselves and their conditions of life by their own
initiative and efforts. The aim of the utilitarians was to clear the
path for individual self-realization. Paine's idea that the community should take positive responsibility for the welfare of its
citizens in the largest sense, for their bodily needs by social
services, for their spiritual needs by an effective educational
system, was altogether opposite in tendency to utilitarian
optimism about the self-redemptive potentialities of the free
individual.

By the middle of the century much of the work of the movement had been done. The reform of parliament, accepted more
in principle than in practice by the Reform Bill of 1832, was more
substantially realized in 1867. The chief representatives of
secular individualism were Mill and Spencer. In the end Mill
came to acknowledge that his paramount aim, the greatest
possible liberation of the human individual, needed to be quali-
fied because of the more or less accidental differences of strength
between individuals, as is shown by his mildly socialistic re-
visions in the later editions of his *Principles of Political Economy*.

Spencer affirmed individualism with uncompromising ferocity. Where Bentham had, broadly speaking, ignored problems of education and social welfare, Spencer explicitly asserted, on the basis of the evolutionary account of the progress of mankind, that any state interference with the natural elimination of weak and uncompetitive individuals would disastrously impede, if not reverse, the ascent of man up the evolutionary scale. 'The survival of the fittest' is, after all, Spencer's phrase. 'The ultimate result of shielding men from folly', he wrote in his *Autobiography*, 'is to fill the world with fools.' The only proper tasks of the state are the repression of violence and the enforcement of contracts. Spencer expressed these views as early as 1843 in his essay on *The Proper Sphere of Government* and held firmly to them until his best-known exposition of them in *Man versus the State* in 1884. With him individualism (and the celebration of industrial society) reaches its greatest intensity. His dissenting origins disposed him against authority; his unimaginative rationalism was enchanted by the brute productiveness of industrial capitalism, while obscuring from him its destructive side-effects; his evolutionary interests enabled him to see unrestricted competitiveness in human society as an application of the law of all progress.

One of Green's most quoted observations is his injunction to his juniors to close up their Mill and Spencer and to turn to Kant and Hegel. In saying this he must have had in mind not merely the empiricism of the British philosophers but also the political individualism of which Hegel's *Philosophy of Right* is a sustained criticism. For Hegel Britain was the paradigm *bürgerliche Gesellschaft* and Mill and Spencer were its prophets at the height of its career. Green exemplified in his own life the ideal of socially responsible politics he propounded in theory. He was a town councillor, the founder of a free secondary school, and an active temperance reformer. When he died he was buried in a municipal cemetery. Collingwood, in his *Autobiography*, says that the Greats school in Oxford under Green's influence, 'was not meant as a training for professional scholars and philosophers; it was meant as a training for public life', that it sent out 'a stream of ex-pupils who carried with them the conviction that philosophy, and in particular the philosophy they had learnt at Oxford, was an important thing and that their vocation was to put it into practice. This conviction was common to politicians so diverse in their creeds as Asquith and Milner, churchmen like Gore and Scott Holland, social reformers like Arnold Toynbee' (p. 17). It was under Asquith's government that the foundations of the modern welfare state were laid. Gore and Scott Holland were leaders of the Christian socialist movement in the Church of England which sought to detach the church from its association with the propertied classes and those bound to them by habitual deference and to involve it constructively in the life of the neglected urban masses.

Green's theoretical and practical commitment to a new view of the state's responsibilities was also to be found in Bosanquet, who was both author of *The Philosophical Theory of the State* (1899) and secretary of the Charity Organization Society. Many followed them in both aspects of this concern for an actively benevolent state. Among lesser idealists Henry Jones wrote *The Working Faith of a Social Reformer* (1916) and *The Principles of Citizenship* (1919), J. H. Muirhead *The Service of the State* (1909), works whose titles clearly declare the social and political attitude expressed in them. Here again, as in the matter of religion, Bradley and McTaggart are exceptions. Bradley's chapter on 'My Station and its Duties' in *Ethical Studies* gives a conservative, hierarchical interpretation to the main themes of the Hegelian theory of politics. McTaggart's chapter on 'the conception of society as an organism' in his *Studies in Hegelian Cosmology* understands that conception in a purely ideal sense: the organic society is realized in the ultimate community of mutually loving immortal souls, not in any historically actual state.

Green's responsible collectivism still exhibited some of the native distrust of state power. (Cf. R. Metz, *A Hundred Years of British Philosophy*, p. 283.) The state cannot make men good, it can only create conditions favourable to their moral perfection of themselves. Yet despite this, and despite his insistence that rights are created not by the politically sovereign power but by the indwelling moral consensus of society, his underlying commitment to the Hegelian idea that the state is an essentially moral institution, absorbing and even superseding the individual morality of its members, comes out in his surprising contention that Czarist Russia is not a state. His famous lecture of 1880, 'Liberal Legislation and Freedom of Contract', opposed the defence of privilege and unequal strength by appeals to liberty. He thought little of the liberty that would be infringed by forbidding tenants to contract away their game-rights to landlords, by limiting the sale of alcoholic drinks, and by compelling employers to assume liability for injuries sustained by their employees. Green argued for these infringements, perhaps questionably, as contributing to a larger general freedom. This way of presenting his ideas made them more acceptable to progressive theorists of liberalism like L. T. Hobhouse, despite his hostility to the Hegelian foundations of Green's concrete political doctrines. It is not fanciful of A. B. Ulam (*Philosophical Foundations of English Socialism*) to see in Green an ancestor of the modern labour party.

IV

A question is raised by the rapidity with which idealism became the dominant philosophical school in British universities. For its success was undoubtedly rapid. In 1865 Stirling communicated his turgid version of the Hegelian message in *The Secret of Hegel*, the first work in English on Hegel that was both detailed and enthusiastic, even if, as I shall show later, Stirling was not by any means the first to bring news of Hegel to Britain. In less than ten years a series of works came out, bearing a strong Hegelian imprint, from those who were to be the leaders and inspirers of a whole generation of British philosophers. For the next thirty years absolute idealism maintained an unchallenged primacy, both in volume of publications and in its hold over the loyalties of university students.

The reasons for this swift conquest are two: first, the debility of the native philosophical tradition, both in the predominant form in which it was radically opposed to idealism and in the form in which it had some broad affinity with it, and secondly the revival of the universities from the torpor of the preceding age. In the 1860s, on the eve of the emergence of idealism, the party-lines in philosophy were much the same as they had been more than twenty years earlier, as described by Mill in his essays on Bentham and Coleridge. The school of experience, of which Mill himself was now the senior luminary, confronted the school of intuition. In the early part of the century the empiricist tradition deriving from Locke and Hume had been most alive in the ethics and psychology of Bentham and James Mill. Although the latter had applied Hume's associationism with mechanical thoroughness to the whole range of mental phenomena, no member of the utilitarian school had addressed himself seriously to epistemological issues before John Stuart Mill and none introduced significant modifications, as Mill did, into the body of inherited empiricist assumptions in this area.

On the other side, the school of intuition to which Mill

referred was the Scottish philosophy of common sense. It had
been initiated by Thomas Reid in the late eighteenth century
as the most respectable of the numerous 'answers to Hume' put
out by his contemporaries. It had been laboriously, if elegantly,
expounded in the writings of Dugald Stewart between 1792 and
his death in 1828. The leadership of the school had then passed
from him to Sir William Hamilton, who replaced Stewart's
polite facility with a vast accumulation of insecure and heavily-
borne learning. Hamilton's ideas were presented in a series of
Edinburgh Review articles between 1829 and 1833. The first was a
metaphysical agnosticism that rested on the thesis that all our
knowledge is inescapably relative and conditioned. Secondly,
Hamilton upheld a 'natural realism' about perception, which he
took to be an immediate awareness of external reality, at least
through the sense of touch. Finally, Hamilton added some fairly
footling amendments and complications to the syllogistic logic
traditionally taught in universities.

Hamilton died in 1856 and from then on the chief exponent
of intuitionism was, until his death in 1871, H. L. Mansel of
Oxford (in his last few years Dean of St. Paul's), the first leading
figure of his school to come from outside its country of origin.
He seems to have left no immediate disciples. Spencer and
G. H. Lewes drew on his conception of the Unknowable to round
out their eclectic and encyclopedic systems. But they did not use
it, as he had, to impose a Kantian limit on the possible scope of
human knowledge so as to leave room for faith. For them it
was at most a respectful gesture towards the idea that natural
science, for all its splendid gifts of enlightenment, cannot answer
all the questions that men feel impelled to raise about the
ultimate nature of things. It could also be seen as an emblem of
the open-ended and incompletable nature of scientific inquiry.

After Mansel's death the Scottish philosophy remained alive
only in the United States, through the influence of James
McCosh, president of Princeton. Calderwood and Veitch were
unable to stem the tide of idealism in Scotland and from Oxford
it appears to have disappeared without trace. Such resistance as
there was in late Victorian Oxford to the school of Green came
from the physical realism of the Aristotelian scholar Thomas
Case and, later, from the pragmatism of F. C. S. Schiller and his
quaint group of associates and from the sporadic critical
activity of Cook Wilson, which was only to take the form of an
articulate philosophical standpoint after the turn of the century
in the work of his pupil Prichard.

By the 1860s, then, the established version of rationalism was, in effect, sustained by one man, Mansel, and after his death soon petered out altogether. Reid had praised Hume for supplying empiricism with a *reductio ad absurdum* by the thoroughness and penetration with which he developed the implications of its assumptions that only ideas, and not real things, are perceived and that the organizing principles of thought are of empirical origin. Against the second assumption he held that the principles of substance, cause, and the like are self-evident *a priori* truths. This theory of first principles resembled Kant's in its results, but it achieved them, not by the honest if exhausting toil of Kantian deduction, but by postulation combined with an appeal to candour. A naïve and diluted Kantianism of this kind could offer no serious resistance to a philosophy such as Hegel's, which started from a reasoned rejection of Kant's findings, in particular of the doctrine of unknowable things-in-themselves, and developed by way of a thorough criticism of the detailed reasoning that Kant had provided for them.

As a general current of thought empiricism, or perhaps one should say naturalism, the philosophy which takes the natural sciences to be the paradigm of human knowledge, received a marked, but somewhat too intoxicating, stimulus from Darwinism. Huxley embraced the doctrines of Hume as a philosophical foundation for his general beliefs; G. H. Lewes those of Auguste Comte. But the richness and variety of the fields which presented themselves as fit for the application of the evolutionary principle (not just organic life but inanimate nature, on the one hand, the mind, morality, and social institutions on the other) caused attention to be drawn away from the more strictly philosophical bases of triumphant naturalism to the more congenial business of finding ever-new confirmations in the world of natural fact for the explanatory power of the new master-principle. The only significant exception to this tendency away from the central and towards the peripheral among naturalistic philosophers of the period is to be found in the work of W. K. Clifford who died in 1879 at the age of thirty-four. Clifford left behind the raw materials for a British equivalent of the philosophy of Mach. In the end this was to be set out systematically by the statistician Karl Pearson in *The Grammar of Science* in 1892.

Now just at the time when the naturalistic philosophy dominant outside the universities was becoming increasingly unphilosophical under the influence of Darwinism and when its rationalistic opponent within the universities was dwindling away, as much, one might feel, from lack of intrinsic intellectual vigour as from a shortage of gifted exponents, the universities themselves were beginning to respond to the effects of reform. The disquiet of the educated public about their ossified condition, in which intellectual weakness and social exclusiveness reinforced each other, had been expressed through the reforming commissions. Against dogged obstruction by the universities themselves the commissions had sought to create an effective professoriate for the sake of improved scholarly standards and to remove barriers to admission, both of teachers and undergraduates, so as to ensure an academic population fitted to sustain and profit by them. Those like Mark Pattison who were most concerned about the low scholarly level of the ancient British universities looked to Germany for their models. It is not surprising that the new philosophical movement should be inspired by the last German philosopher about whose classical status there was broad agreement in his own country. There is a certain irony in the fact that Hamilton, whose philosophy was completely swept away from the intellectual scene of Oxford after reform, had been the most vehement propagandist for change. The effective chairs for which he had called so stridently were to be occupied by Hegelians who had no use for him.

In a cursory survey like this it is easy to exaggerate the changes brought about by a reforming movement. Oxford in the early nineteenth century had not been the Oxford of Gibbon's and Bentham's scornful recollections, even less, no doubt, than eighteenth-century Oxford had been. The general level of academic work had been raised by the introduction of competitive, or, at any rate, classified, examinations and the stimulation of serious effort among the taught had not gone without a response from their teachers. The circle of Noëtics at Oriel in the 1830s, led by Whately, had been an indication of intellectual vitality among the younger fellows of colleges. But Whately, although a clever and intellectually vigorous man, had no substantial new doctrine to teach. His logic, somewhat like that of Ramus, had been more a removal of petrified complications than a really new forward movement. Furthermore Whately's initiative had had an altogether too disturbing outcome. The one really major intelligence among his pupils had been that of Newman. The result of the Oxford movement was that its adherents either joined the Roman church and left the university altogether or retreated into a frightened or taciturn conformity about fundamental questions. But twenty years after, in the

1860s, the distrust in the free play of mind engendered by this episode was beginning to dissipate.

V

British idealism is commonly assumed to be largely Hegelian in inspiration. Although this assumption has been questioned, it is, as I shall argue later, substantially correct. The unsurprising facts that the British idealists were by no means unselective in their attitude to their German master and that they had ideas of their own to develop within the framework with which he provided them do not undermine it. It is, at any rate, clear that they owed more to Hegel than to anyone else.

I have argued that Hegelianism was appropriate to religious and political needs present in the 1860s and 1870s, and that its success here was accelerated by a lack of competition from a moribund intuitionism which had no political implications and underwrote a bleakly authoritarian and fideistic attitude to religion and from a naturalism that, intoxicated with Darwin, was ignoring fundamental issues about scientific knowledge for the more agreeable task of systematizing and extrapolating from the findings of science.

These considerations do not wholly answer the question of why it was not until more than thirty years after his death that Hegel should receive serious study and endorsement in Britain. In Germany by the 1840s the Hegelian school had disintegrated. By the mid 1860s it was alive only as a style in the history of philosophy, as practised by Erdmann, Zeller, and Kuno Fischer. In 1865, the year of Stirling's excited welcome to Hegel, Liebmann was issuing the call of 'back to Kant' which was to be the slogan of most academic philosophizing in Germany until well after the end of the century.

The explanation needed is, however, implicit in what has been said about the state of British philosophy in the early part of the nineteenth century. Poor communications with the philosophy of the outside world were the result of the parochialism, inertia, and markedly practical bias of the British philosophy of the age. There is a striking contrast between the speed with which knowledge of Kant became available in this country as compared with that of Hegel. Introductory expositions of and selections from Kant's writings were published in Britain in the 1790s, a decade after the first edition of the *Critique of Pure*

Reason and a decade before Kant's death in 1804. The only reference in British philosophical writing to Hegel before his death in 1831 is to be found in Hamilton's essay on 'The Philosophy of the Unconditioned' in 1829 and there he is mentioned only in passing, along with Oken, as one of the distinguished followers of Schelling (*Discussions*, p. 21).

Eight years earlier, in a supplementary dissertation to the *Encyclopaedia Britannica*, recounting the history of philosophy in Europe since the revival of letters, Dugald Stewart makes no mention of Hegel, although, after some vapid remarks about Kant, he stigmatizes the doctrines of Fichte and Schelling as 'sad aberrations of human reason', despite admitting that he cannot make anything of Fichte and cannot read German anyway. The translation in 1832 of the abridgement of Tennemann's history of philosophy gave some account of Hegel's views. But it was not until 1846 that a fairly reasonable account of the main outlines of Hegel's system came from a British writer, in J. D. Morell's book on recent European philosophy. Morell is lumped together with his quite hopeless near-contemporary Robert Blakey (who made some vague remarks about Hegel in the fourth volume of his *History of the Philosophy of Mind* in 1850) by Muirhead as exemplifying the theological prejudice which blinded the eyes of British readers to the illumination available to them in the works of the German idealists. The entirely reasonable comments on Hegel by Morell which provoke this condemnation are that in his system 'theism . . . is compromised . . . the hope of immortality likewise perishes . . . religion, if not destroyed by the Hegelian philosophy, is absorbed in it'. The objection that Hegel is altogether too costly a defender of religion in divesting man of immortality and God of both personality and real transcendence is precisely that voiced by Pringle-Pattison and a host of other personal idealists after him against both Hegel and Bradley.

Morell, who had studied philosophy at Bonn in the early 1840s and whose subsequent career as an inspector of schools is approximately contemporary with that of Matthew Arnold, gives a reasonably detailed, accurate, and intelligible account of the main ingredients of Hegel's system and of the dialectic which is its generating principle. Anyone interested by what he had to say about Hegel must have been led to share his theological disquiet by another publication in the same year which was of ultimately Hegelian ancestry: Strauss's *Leben Jesu*, translated into English by George Eliot.

In 1844, two years before Morell's book, Jowett had made a visit to Germany with A. P. Stanley, largely for purposes of philosophical study. By 1845 he was writing about the study of Hegel, 'one must go on or perish in the attempt, that is to say, give up Metaphysics altogether. It is impossible to be satisfied with any other system after you have begun with this.' Jowett's biographers, Abbott and Campbell, report that he and Temple began a translation of Hegel's 'logic' (they do not say whether it was the greater or the smaller one) but that in 1849 it was 'broken off by Temple's being summoned away to public life' (Abbott and Campbell, vol. i, p. 129). 'Hegel is a great book', they report Jowett as saying, 'if you can only get it out of its dialectical form.' He had a high regard for Hegel as a critic of Greek philosophy and said 'the study of Hegel has given me a method'. Metz and Faber are surely right in ascribing to Jowett a large part of the responsibility for the effective introduction of Hegel's thought into this country. Even if he did it through teaching and conversation rather than writing books, the people he taught, above all Green and Caird, were those who were to establish the school of Absolute Idealism.

Jowett's attitude to Hegel itself underwent a dialectical change. By the 1870s, suspicious of the effect of Green's earnest obscurities on the undergraduates of Balliol, he was complaining that 'metaphysics exercise a fatal influence over the mind'. But by 1884, accepting the gift of a bust of Hegel for the Balliol library from Lord Arthur Russell, he adopted a more favourable posture. 'Though not a Hegelian', he wrote, 'I think I have gained more from Hegel than from any other philosopher.' Of the bust itself he added, 'Hegel looks quite a gentleman'. We may perhaps see this as a symbol of the satisfactory absorption of Hegelianism into British intellectual life.

Hamilton returned to Hegel in 1852, when preparing his early essays for publication as a book. In a massive footnote to his essay of 1829 he objected to the dialectic as founded 'on a mistake in logic and a violation of logic' (*Discussions*, p. 24). In an appendix on 'Oxford as it might be', he says: 'I have never, in fact, met with a Hegelian (and I have known several of distinguished talents, both German and British) who could answer three questions, without being driven to the confession that he did not, as yet, fully *comprehend* the doctrine of his master, though *believing* it to be all true.' It would be interesting to know who the distinguished British Hegelians of the early 1850s were, but Hamilton was never much obsessed with mere fact.

Like his further remark, 'I am told that Hegelianism is making way at Oxford', it may be an echo of Jowett's teaching.

At this time two independent British philosophers of an idealist tendency, critical both of Mill's empiricism and the Hamiltonian philosophy which opposed it, were active: J. F. Ferrier in Scotland, whose main work *The Institutes of Metaphysic* came out in 1854, and John Grote of Cambridge, whose scattered and somewhat desultory writings on the theory of knowledge appeared in the two volumes of *Exploratio Philosophica*, the first in 1865 a year before his death, the second not until 1900.

Ferrier, according to G. E. Davie's well-documented account in *The Democratic Intellect*, was a dissident Hamiltonian, provoked into speculative extravagance more by his hostility to evangelical pressures against freedom than by any positive affinity to German idealism (he described his own, rather Berkeleyan, philosophy as 'Scottish to the core') or, for that matter, by much knowledge of it. He wrote a short note about Hegel for a biographical dictionary in the late 1850s. Perhaps his relation to Hegel is best brought out by a story of Stirling's who 'found him diligently engaged on a work of Hegel which turned out to be upside down. Ferrier's explanation was that being utterly baffled in the attempt to understand his author the right side up, he tried the other way in desperation' (Davie, op. cit., p. 335). There is only a single reference to Hegel in Grote in which he is mentioned, along with Schelling, as an object of such distaste to Mill as to bring him into agreement with Hamilton on a certain point.

Before Stirling's book, then, although it was possible to find a short but not too cursory account of Hegel's philosophy in Morell, and from 1855 a translation of the Subjective Logic, brought into English by way of a French version of the original, the only really effective presentation of Hegel's ideas must have been in the personal teaching of Jowett. By 1860, the year Green became a fellow of Balliol, another Oxford philosopher, Hamilton's follower Mansel, gave a competent survey of Hegel's ideas in half a dozen pages of his *Metaphysics*, whose footnotes make clear his direct acquaintance with Hegel's text. It was in Oxford at any rate that the chief exponent of Absolute Idealism in Scotland, Edward Caird, acquired the views which, from his appointment in 1866 to the moral philosophy chair in Glasgow, he was to present to his fellow Scotsmen and which soon came to dominate the philosophy teaching of the Scottish universities.

Jowett, it would seem, had prepared the ground in such a way that Stirling's book, instead of sinking into the oblivion to which its bizarre and tumultuous style might have destined it, was able to exert a serious influence.

VI

The view that British idealism is a late flowering of the philosophy of Hegel is sometimes challenged in an author-itative-seeming way. The point can be made with examples involving the three chief leaders of the school. Green is quoted as saying 'I looked into Hegel the other day and found it a strange *Wirrwarr*'. Taken by itself this suggests unfamiliarity with, as well as incomprehension of, Hegel. It is pointed out that Caird wrote a massive two-volume work on Kant, and republished it in a substantially revised form twelve years later, but produced only a small, and to a considerable extent bio-graphical, book on Hegel. As for Bradley, there is Collingwood's description of his books as 'criticisms of Mill's logic, Bain's psychology and Mansel's metaphysics by a man whose mind was the most deeply critical that European philosophy has produced since Hume, and whose intention, like that of Locke, was to make a bonfire of rubbish' (*Autobiography*, p. 16).

In fact Green's remark about 'looking into Hegel' comes from some recollections of him by Henry Sidgwick (in *Mind* for 1901). In the paragraph in which it occurs Sidgwick writes, '"Hege-lian" is a term that I should never have applied to the author of the *Prolegomena to Ethics*'. He goes on, 'I think, indeed, that the term might be defended in relation to some of his earlier utter-ances; and that his thought during his life moved away from Hegel. . . . I remember writing to him after a visit to Berlin in 1870 and expressing a desire to "get away from Hegel"; he replied that it seemed to him one might as well try to "get away from thought itself".' So all that is shown is that Green came to think of himself in later years as free from his early dependence on Hegel. As for Caird's concentration on Kant, it must be made clear that he subjects Kant throughout to criticism from a Hegelian point of view and singles out for acceptance from the former just what is absorbed into the philosophy of the latter.

Collingwood's thesis about Bradley is a little more com-plicated. It comes as part of a general endorsement of the idealists' repudiation of the description of them as Hegelians. If 'they had some knowledge of Hegel', he says, they had 'a good deal more of Kant. The fact of their having this knowledge was used by their opponents, more through ignorance than deliberate dishonesty, to discredit them in the eyes of a public always contemptuous of foreigners.' Green, Collingwood goes on, 'had read Hegel in youth but rejected him in middle age; the philosophy he was working out when his early death interrupted him is best described, if a brief description is needed, as a reply to Herbert Spencer by a profound student of Hume'. Collingwood's reference to the national suspicion of foreigners is significant. Writing as almost the last member of the Idealistic rearguard and during the inter-war period when Hegel was widely regarded as somehow responsible for the German aggression of 1914, as in Hobhouse's indictment *The Metaphysical Theory of the State*, he was anxious to clear his predecessors of war-guilt by association. In general Collingwood's sporadically brilliant works abound with shrill assertions of false or dubious statements about matters of fact which he found annoying.

A much more sensible view is to be found in the remarks by Edward Caird on the subject in his introduction to the *Essays in Philosophical Criticism*, which Green's admirers brought out as a memorial to him in 1883, the year after his death. 'To Hegel', Caird said of Green, 'he latterly stood in a somewhat doubtful relation; for while, in the main, he accepted Hegel's criticism of Kant, and held also that something *like* Hegel's idealism must be the result of the development of Kantian principles rightly understood, he yet regarded the actual Hegelian system with a certain suspicion as something too ambitious, or, at least, premature. "It must all be done again", he once said' (*Essays in Philosophical Criticism*, p. 5).

It is undoubtedly true that no British idealist stood in the kind of discipular relation to Hegel which the more authoritative type of philosopher regards as a criterion of really understanding his message. Such subservience usually presupposes personal contact, which was chronologically ruled out in this case. Nobody, in other words, swallowed Hegel whole. But there is, after all, a great deal of Hegel to swallow. In particular the dialectic, conceived in Hegel's way, as a rigorous and systematically deductive ordering of all the categories from being and not-being, through the abstractions of logic and the increasingly concrete notions of nature and spirit, to terminate in the absolute idea, is nowhere embraced in the work of a British idealist. McTaggart took it seriously enough to devote his first book to a scrupulously rational criticism of its detailed workings. Bradley's distantly respectful attitude is more typical of the movement. In *The Principles of Logic* he writes: 'I need hardly say that it is not my intention comprehensively to dispose in a single paragraph of a system which, with all its shortcomings, has been worked over as wide an area of experience as any system offered in its place' (p. 147). Again, he says: 'In this speculative movement, if we take it in the character it claims for itself, I neither myself profess belief nor ask it from the reader' (p. 189). The most he will do is to 'profess that the individual is the identity of universal and particular' (ibid.). Even the devoted Stirling is assailed by doubt when he contemplates the ceremonial elaboration of the dialectic: 'the fact is, it is all maundering, but with the most audacious usurpation of author-itative speech on the mysteries that must remain mysteries' (*The Secret of Hegel*, vol. i, p. 73).

The British idealists were not, then, slavish adherents of Hegel in all the detailed effrontery of his system. They were thoroughly selective in their approach to him and they had original ideas of their own as well as original applications of his principles to contribute. But it is implausible to suggest, as Collingwood comes near to doing, that their philosophy is an original native growth. In Caird's words they 'agree in believing that the line of investigation which philosophy must follow . . . is that which was opened up by Kant, and for the successful prosecution of which no one has done so much as Hegel'. If Coleridge was chiefly influenced by Schelling and Carlyle by Fichte, the professional philosophers owed little or nothing to either and made neg-ligible reference to them. The only serious alternative to Hegel as the chief influence on their thought is Kant.

Although a certain community of basic vocabulary between Kant and Hegel may at first glance suggest that it is an open question which of the two the idealists most closely adhere to, brief reflection is sufficient to show beyond doubt that they are essentially Hegelian in their views about both reality and knowledge. In Kant's view ultimate reality, the realm of nou-mena, is unknowable by the human mind, except, inconsistently, in the three respects that it exists, that it contains a mental as well as a non-mental aspect and, by implication, that the latter exercises some kind of determining influence on the sensory raw material which it is the business of the understanding to articulate into knowledge. For all his condemnation of tran-scendent metaphysics, Kant is himself, marginally but essentially, a practitioner of the forbidden art. Hegel, on the other hand, recognizes Kant's inconsistency about the transcendent nature of reality and overcomes the difficulty by taking reality, in the form of his Absolute, to be, not something altogether beyond experience and of a wholly different nature from it, but as a logically ideal completion or totality of experience. In this respect the British idealists follow Hegel exactly.

The point is clearly made in a remark of Green's I have quoted before: 'there is one spiritual self-conscious being of which all that is real is the activity and expression, . . . we are related to this spiritual being, not merely as parts of the world which is its expression, but as partakers in some inchoate measure of the self-consciousness through which it at once constitutes itself and distinguishes itself from the world' (*Works*, vol. iii, p. 143). In less ethereal terms, our minds and their experiences are not cut off from reality itself, but are, somehow, parts of it. Bradley, again, does not take reality, the harmonious absolute experience that lies above the level of relations, to be something quite distinct from the appearances which are the objects of discursive thought. For him appearances are all constitutive parts of reality; indeed he suggests that reality is nothing more than the totality of appearances, harmonized into a fully rational system. For the British idealists, as for Hegel, there is only one world, which we apprehend with varying degrees of adequacy, from the crude intimations of sense at one extreme to the absolute knowledge of philosophy at the other. For Kant, on the other hand, there are two worlds, quite distinct from each other; the unknowable or barely knowable order of noumena and the order of phenomena, jointly produced by sensation and the understanding.

The epistemological affinities of British idealism are equally Hegelian rather than Kantian. For Kant there are three distinct faculties involved in our acquisition of knowledge, or our claims to it, at any rate: sense, understanding, and reason. Sense is a passive receptivity and, by itself, is disorderly and inarticulate. Only if its deliverances are synthesized by the understanding can we achieve objective knowledge of phenomena, material or mental. In reason the intellect is exercised independently of the sensations which are the indispensable content for its formative activity. The result is transcendent metaphysics, not knowledge at all, but only a delusive chimera, a 'natural and unavoidable illusion' (*Critique of Pure Reason*, A 298, B 354). Reason is dialectical, then, where this means that 'we conclude from something which we know to something else of which have no concept, and to which, owing to an inevitable illusion, we yet ascribe objective reality' (ibid., A 339, B 397). Its arguments are 'sophisms, not of men, but of pure reason itself'.

Hegel, of course, reverses Kant's comparative estimate of understanding and reason. Understanding, operating in accordance with the fixed principles of formal logic, yields us knowledge of an inferior sort in common life and the sciences, knowledge that is abstract, partial, and deficient. True knowledge is only to be obtained by the employment of philosophic reason, in accordance with the principles of the dialectic. Reason is not the source of errors which, just because so natural and interesting to us, have to be rooted out; it is the only discoverer of ultimate truth. If ultimate reality were, as Kant supposes, noumenal, then reason, with its dialectical procedure, would be delusive. But, in Hegel's view reality is not noumenal; it is, rather, total, infinite, and all-inclusive, and only the dialectical reason of philosophy, apprehending it as a harmonious and unitary system, can give us genuine knowledge of it as it really is and that surpasses the abstraction and limitedness of the understanding.

In this conception of the nature, object, and cognitive potentialities of reason as compared with understanding the British idealists are at one with Hegel. They agree that since reality is not noumenal, not transcendent of experience, reason can give knowledge of it. Where they differ from Hegel is in regard to the supposition that the philosopher, armed with all the powers of reason, can apply it to provide a detailed, systematic, and demonstratively rigorous account of reality as a whole in which are finally ordered all the partial apprehensions of reality through which we progressively approximate to a true and absolute knowledge of it. That is what is meant by Green's remark that it must all be done again. It is the point of Bradley's repeated insistence that we can be sure that all the disharmonies of appearance are *somehow* reconciled in the absolute. The British idealists suspect the presumption with which Hegel applies his leading principles to the detail of the world and thought. But they unreservedly endorse the principles themselves.

VII

There is a comical immodesty about the titles G. E. Moore gave to the two influential works he published in 1903. It is more obvious in the case of *Principia Ethica* with its implied comparison with Newton's masterpiece. But there is a measure of presumption also in the title of his essay of that year: *The Refutation of Idealism*. It lies not so much in the claim, which Moore himself soon abandoned, to have succeeded in the work of refutation but rather in the supposition that the doctrine to which he was objecting, Berkeley's principle that to be is to be perceived, is the essence of idealism. For it was Hegel's, not Berkeley's, idealism that was a live issue at the time he was writing. If the Hegelian philosophy had a slogan it was rather that all reality is spiritual in nature or, even more fundamentally, that there is no truth or being short of truth and reality as a whole.

Russell's essay on *The Nature of Truth* which came out three years later supplies a more perceptive account of the main theme of idealism. He begins by objecting to the coherence theory of truth, in Joachim's version, that it is self-refuting. The thesis that nothing short of the whole truth is more than partially true is itself less than the whole truth. But he does not confine himself to this kind of direct criticism of the coherence theory. He goes on to say: 'the doctrines we have been considering may all be deduced from one central logical doctrine, which may be expressed thus: "every relation is grounded in the natures of the related term". Let us call this the *axiom of internal relations*' (*Philosophical Essays*, rev. edn. p. 139).

One way of showing that Russell's account of the theoretical core of absolute idealism is preferable to Moore's is by considering the main issues with which the idealists actually concerned themselves. Green's lengthy critique of Hume is preoccupied with Hume's atomism, with his conception of reality as an aggregate of items of feeling or sensation, externally related to one another. The same theme is pursued positively in the early, metaphysical, part of his *Prolegomena to Ethics*. Bradley's main object in the first, critical, part of *Appearance and Reality* is to show the incoherent, contradictory character of the categories of the understanding of discursive or relational thought. The central argument here is that the understanding falls into contradiction by seeking to conceive reality as a complex of things that are at once distinct from each other and from the relations between them.

Another consideration that supports the view that the principle of internal relations is fundamental to idealism is that all the more specific doctrines of the school can be seen as applications of it to comparatively specific problems. Five of these applications are fairly comprehensive.

(1) The first is monism, in Spinoza's sense, the theory that there is only one true substance, the absolute or reality as a whole. It follows from the basic principle, together with the reasonable assumption that everything is related, directly or indirectly, to everything else. It is perhaps most plausible in the causal form given to it by Blanshard (*Nature of Thought*, chaps. 31 and 32). If causality is more than regular succession, it seems it can only be some kind of logical relation of entailment. So, if all events are causally related, they are also all internally related.

(2) The second is the coherence theory of truth. A proposition cannot be considered as true on its own, abstracted from its involvement with other propositions. Furthermore, a proposition cannot be conceived as externally related to the equally abstract fact that the correspondence theory supposes to verify it. The terms of the truth-relation must be systematic and possess a community of character. Proposition and fact are both abstractions from the judgement, understood as a kind of assertive experience, and the ultimate bearer of truth is the total system of coherent judgements which is also the system of experiences that constitutes the world.

(3) The third is the theory of the concrete universal which is put forward to replace the Aristotelian conception of an object as the instantiation by a bare particular of a cluster of abstract universals.

(4) The fourth is the thesis that reality is essentially mental or spiritual in nature. There are two ways in which the doctrine of internal relations supports this conclusion. On the one hand minds are more real, and so more adequate paradigms of reality itself, than material things, because they are more rational and unitary systems. On the other, there is the consideration that thought and being are not distinct and externally related, an idea intimated by the coherence theory of truth.

(5) The fifth application of the doctrine of internal relations is the theory that mind and its objects are internally and thus necessarily related, a particular version of which is the object of Moore's polemic.

There are further, more particular applications of the principle in the fields of art, politics, and religion. In each case the understanding is seen as operating with incoherent abstractions which it is the task of reason to supersede: form and content, state and citizen, the divine and the human.

This system of ideas certainly satisfies two of its own criteria of adequacy. On the one hand it is extremely comprehensive: all sides of human experience, all objects of human interest, except, perhaps, mathematics and natural science, are catered for within it. On the other it is highly systematic and internally coherent. In each of its applications the basic principle of idealism is used to reject an opposition of diverse abstractions developed by the understanding and to establish in its place a concrete and internally related system, which, in its freedom from inner contradiction, is acceptable to reason.

The enchantment of the doctrine is plain enough. But is that a sufficient reason for accepting it? It is clearly not a correct account of the conceptions of things with which we actually think. What is necessarily true of, and thus internal to, an object is, as is often pointed out, relative to the sense of the description we choose to identify it with. As things are none of our descriptions of things involves a conception of their total nature, of everything that is true of them. Our conceptions of individual things are not Leibnizian individual concepts. Critics of the doctrine usually go on at this point to add that the choice between alternative identifying descriptions of a thing is in the end arbitrary. Things have no essences for nothing is internal to the thing itself.

Yet, on the other hand, it is easy to see the attraction of the idea that the fullest possible description of a thing, the one that implies everything that is true of it, is the best or most adequate description of it there could be. To some extent, indeed, the advance of our knowledge of the world seems to confirm this idea. The concepts of science, for example, imply more about the things they identify than the concepts of common observation, which contribute to their development. But the supposition that this process could, in principle, ever be completed is highly questionable. To know everything about anything, as the idealists themselves would admit, must be to know everything about everything. But even if this goal were in principle one that could be achieved, there can be no short cut to it as the doctrine of the cognitive superiority of the reason assumes. It is only by the patient accumulations of the understanding that our conceptions can be enriched.

THE GOOD SELF AND THE BAD SELF:
THE MORAL PSYCHOLOGY OF BRITISH IDEALISM AND THE ENGLISH SCHOOL OF PSYCHOANALYSIS COMPARED

By RICHARD WOLLHEIM

SOME of you may think that in my choice of topic this evening I owe my distinguished predecessor in the chair of philosophy at University College London an apology. For the Dawes Hicks Lecture is a lecture in the history of philosophy, and the thought would be that in taking philosophy to include moral psychology I am obviously at fault for I have violated well-established frontiers. If I choose not to answer such a charge directly, one reason is this: that, rigidly delineated though such frontiers may be, the arguments in support of their being drawn as they are vary considerably. Another reason is that perhaps the best answer to the charge is the indirect answer: so that instead of disputing where the frontiers should run, one is more profitably engaged in showing how the existing lines may be safely transgressed, or, indeed, how in some historical phase progress was made in despite of them, which could not have been achieved if they had been held in respect. But if there is to be even the hope that the history of philosophy can in this way give anything to philosophy, it follows that it must not begin by borrowing from philosophy too rigid or exclusive a conception of what philosophy is. So I remain unapologetic in my choice of topic.

Idealism and psychoanalysis may seem an incongruous pair. The history of their transplantation to Britain is, it is true, in many ways a history of common experience. Originating in the German-speaking world, both encountered fierce opposition on arrival in this country. In the course of time both gained exponents, adherents, disciples, some of great distinction, but in neither case more than (comparatively) a few. And yet both have been held responsible for a wide range of nefarious consequences: intellectual, ethical, social, and practical. But this evening I want to draw your attention to another feature that transplanted idealism and transplanted psychoanalysis have in common. For if we look at the work of their most eminent representatives—and I shall confine myself to the ideas of F. H. Bradley and Melanie Klein—we can, I suggest, discern a joint contribution that they make to the understanding of moral phenomena: a contribution which at once belongs to moral psychology and justifies the claim of moral psychology to be a philosophical discipline.

II

Bradley's *Ethical Studies* is divided into seven essays. Too many readers of the book—barely a class with a superfluity of members —hasten to identify Bradley's own ethical views with the heavily collectivist theory which he expounds in Essay V under the Hegelian heading, 'My Station and its Duties'. They do this, despite the fact that in the very first sentence of the next essay Bradley says of this theory that 'however true'—which is his way of saying 'however many truths it may contain'—it provides 'no sufficient answer to the question What is Morality?'[1] This remark, however, is lost on them for by this time they have brought their reading of Bradley to a close and shut the book.

Such precipitance on the reader's part is unfortunate, and unfortunate for two reasons, which are connected. Already in Essay II Bradley had introduced his own ethical theory. 'The final end', he had written there, 'with which morality is identified, or under which it is included, can be expressed not otherwise than by self-realization'.[2] But it is not until Essay VII that a full-scale account of the theory of self-realization is given, and by stopping short where he does the precipitate reader deprives himself of this. But he also deprives himself of a proper understanding of Bradley's criticisms of alternative ethical theories, given in Essays III and IV, which he will have already read, and is certain to have admired. And the connection is this: that in criticizing Hedonistic theory and Deontological theory Bradley concentrates on the account that each theory provides of moral action, and why moral action, and therefore an adequate account of it, are of supreme importance to ethical theory, becomes fully clear if, and is not obvious unless, one entertains, if not assertorically at least hypothetically, the theory of self-realization.

Indeed this last point, as an observation on Bradley's procedure, could be expressed more forcefully. For it would be little

[1] F. H. Bradley, *Ethical Studies* (Oxford, 2nd edn. 1927), p. 214.
[2] Ibid., p. 81.

exaggeration to say that in criticizing the theory of Pleasure for Pleasure's Sake or the theory of Duty for Duty's Sake—as he calls them—Bradley in effect criticizes each not so much as an ethical theory in its own right but rather as an interpretation of the theory of self-realization. Now if this is so, it follows that the crucial question that Bradley has to ask of each theory is, Does it properly exhibit moral action as self-realization?

Should we now wonder why Bradley proceeds in this way, the answer would seem to lie in something that he says in the course of introducing his own theory. He was, he conceded, in no position, metaphysically that is, to prove the theory. And he went on, 'All that we can do is partially to explain it, and try to render it plausible.'[1] The partial explanation unfolds in two stages. The first stage consists in looking at what can be gathered from alternative ethical theories—or, more strictly, from the accounts of moral action that they provide—about self-realization, and thus seeing what there is that remains to be said. And the second stage consists in the appeal to moral psychology. And as for rendering his theory plausible, Bradley's hope is that plausibility will attach to the theory as the explanation unfolds.

If we make our start with Bradley's criticisms of alternative theory, a preliminary is to recognize the requirement that he places upon an account of moral action: a requirement which derives from the view that he takes of action in general. For Bradley all action is intentional in a fairly strong sense in that we cannot be said to *do* anything that we did not intend to do: though, of course, our actions may fall short of our intentions— we may not do what we intended to do. So, if, for instance, moral action is, as Bradley maintains, self-realization, what it is not is, amongst other things, action in which the self is realized fortuitously or coincidentally. There must be some corresponding idea or set of ideas under which the action was done. It follows from this that, if an ethical theory is to attain to adequacy, it must provide an account of moral action that assigns to it the appropriate intentionality: or, to use language that is peculiarly appropriate to Bradley's thinking, the theory must capture the volitional structure of moral action.

So the first question to be asked is, Does Hedonism do this? Now, according to Bradley it is characteristic of authentic Hedonistic theory—that is, theory at once consistent and consistently Hedonistic, of which he thought that, avowals to the contrary, there was precious little around—that it presents

[1] Ibid., p. 65.

the moral agent thus: that on each and every occasion that he acts morally, he wills some particular pleasure. He wills, in other words (the gloss is Bradley's, and we shall see its significance), 'a state of the feeling self'.[1] If such a man's will is invariably actualized, it follows that his existence will unfold as a succession of pleasurable states. Now, if we ask whether such a succession amounts to self-realization, the answer must depend on the relations between the various pleasurable states— whether, that is, they fit together into, or form, a pattern or whole: and since there is nothing in the Hedonistic account of what the man wills that corresponds to such an outcome, that account as an account of moral action must be defective. For it to be adequate to the intentionality of moral action it must ascribe to the moral agent not only the idea of this or that particular end but also some general standing idea under which he wills the end he does.

If Hedonistic theory is thus deficient, the second question to be asked is, Does Deontological theory show us how to repair this deficiency? According to Bradley it is characteristic of this theory that it presents the moral agent thus: that on each and every occasion that he acts morally, he wills to act under one and the same idea which is also of the greatest generality. The idea under which he wills may be called—'indifferently' Bradley says[2]—Freedom, Universality, Autonomy, or the Formal Will. But the trouble with this idea, it would seem, is that, in any of its guises, it goes too far—it goes all the way, we might say—in the direction of generality. Bradley characterizes it as 'mere universal', and what he means by this might be put by saying that the agent may quite properly be said to be able to will anything under it, alternatively to will nothing under it. Anything: in that any particular end is compatible with it. Nothing: in that no particular end is indicated by it. If what is wrong with Hedonism is that, if the moral agent wills as the account it provides specifies, and his will is actualized, he will not necessarily achieve self-realization, what is wrong with Deontological theory is that, if the agent wills as the account it provides specifies, there is no clear sense that can be given to supposing that his will is or indeed could be actualized. Of no one particular action rather than another can it be said, as needs to be said, that *it* matches his intention.

However, to put the matter so might suggest that, at any

[1] Ibid., p. 94.
[2] Ibid., p. 144.

rate on the present showing, Hedonistic theory has for Bradley a start over Deontological theory as an interpretation of the theory of self-realization. For, whatever else self-realization may be, it is surely action—it is, in Bradley's words, a 'doing',[1] a 'putting forth'[2]—and, this being so, must it not be for him a relative merit of Hedonistic theory that it assigns to the moral agent a volitional structure from which some kind of action could follow, and, equally, a relative demerit of Deontological theory that from the volitional structure it assigns him no action could conceivably follow? But Bradley does not think like this. He does not allow Hedonistic theory even a temporary advantage over Deontological theory, and we must try to see why. It is certainly true that Hedonistic theory assigns to the moral agent an intentionality from which action could ensue, but Bradley's point is the action that ensues or would ensue is quite improperly related—improperly, that is, from the point of view of a theory of moral action—to that intentionality. It is related as means to end, so that, for instance, if a better means were found to the same end, that should be preferred as a way of realizing that intention. But it is a requirement on moral action not only (as we have seen) that the action should not be fortuitous, that is that there should be an intention, but also that the action should not be merely instrumentally related to the intention: the end should be realized not merely through the action but in the action. But, if the end is, as Hedonistic theory would have it, a particular state of the feeling self—just that—this requirement cannot, in the nature of that end, be satisfied. So, to adapt a distinction of Bradley's: at best Hedonistic theory could offer an ethic of self-realizedness, not—which is what we are after—an ethic of self-realization.

A good and natural way of expressing Bradley's criticisms of these alternative theories would be to say that each theory is one-sided. And this is just what Bradley says.[3] But when he says it, he wants the phrase to be taken—well, if not literally, then at any rate as a living, rather than as a dead, metaphor. For it is for Bradley a truth, a theoretical truth, about volition that it has two 'sides', a universal side and a particular side,[4] a truth which he thinks is displayed in, or which we can grasp through, the very form of the assertion 'I will this or that', for in saying

---

[1] Ibid., p. 65.
[2] Ibid., pp. 66, 267.
[3] Ibid., p. 142.
[4] Ibid., pp. 72–3.

this we mean (and I quote) 'to distinguish the self, as will in general, from this or that object of desire'.[1] Accordingly, a theory which is to go beyond Hedonistic theory and Deontological theory must afford full recognition to both sides of moral volition, and in doing so it must, of course, repair those injustices which each side has suffered from the theory that recognizes it exclusively. And then it must do something which in the nature of the case neither of the alternative theories could even attempt: it must exhibit how in moral action the two sides are brought into relation. It is just this additional task that I had in mind when I talked of the appositeness of the phrase 'volitional structure' to Bradley's form of ethical inquiry.

What Bradley has then to do for his ethical theory is to show what the particular end is in moral volition, what the self is in moral volition, and how it is that the two are brought into conjunction so that the latter realizes itself in willing the former. It is in pursuit of such an account that Bradley turns away from existing ethical theory to psychology, and we thus enter upon the second stage in his partial explanation of what he regards as true ethical theory. The two stages are related thus: that, having gained from alternative philosophical theory the general form of moral volition, Bradley looks to psychology to inform him about its content, and when he has, as it were, placed one inside the other, he will then be able to say what the volitional structure of moral action is. He will still not have proved his ethical theory but he may have made it seem more plausible against our moral intuitions, and, in doing so, he will, with luck, have sharpened them.

III

Bradley's appeal to psychology starts not with the complex phenomenon of moral action but with about the simplest type of action that can be said to have a volitional structure. Its simplicity Bradley takes as showing that it possesses not only logical priority, but also temporal priority in the history of the individual. His name for it is 'appetite', and his account, which is to be found in Essay VII of *Ethical Studies*, 'Selfishness and Self-Sacrifice', runs as follows:

An agent perceives a sensuous thing, which he subsumes under one idea or more. His condition is such that the idea of this thing, or perhaps better, the idea of having the thing, arouses in him a complex of feelings. On the one hand, he experiences a painful

[1] Ibid., p. 71.

feeling, connected with the fact that he does not have, or that he lacks, the thing—a feeling which may, or may not, be a continuation of existent want. On the other hand, he experiences a pleasurable feeling, because the having of the thing is somehow connected for him with satisfaction. The two feelings, pain and pleasure, set up a tension, and the felt tension, otherwise called desire, moves the agent to have the thing.[1] An example: A small child sees and recognizes a lump of sugar. His condition is such that the thought of not having the sugar excites in him feelings of hunger. And it is also such that the thought of having the sugar excites in him feelings that would accompany his eating sugar. The first experience is painful, the second pleasurable, and the conjunction leads him to reach out a hand for the sugar or to cry for it.

If we now ask what the content of the volitional structure is in this case, we get this answer: The particular side, or end, is represented by the idea of the sensuous thing. The universal side or self is represented by the pleasure that is excited by the idea of the thing and that moves the agent towards the thing itself. And the two sides are related through physical want.

An instant way of bringing this account into focus, or of holding it steady, is to concentrate on the role it assigns to pleasure, and then to contrast this with the role that pleasure has assigned to it in a typically Hedonistic account of action. What does this allow us to see? In the first place, on the present account pleasure does not appear at all on the particular side, which in the Hedonistic account it monopolizes: what is willed is now willed under the idea of a particular thing, not of a particular pleasure. And, secondly, where pleasure does appear on this account—that is, on the universal side—it is pleasure itself that appears there, not the idea of pleasure, which is all that the Hedonistic account lets in: this, according to Bradley, must be right, for, at any rate in the ordinary kind of case, it is only feeling, of which pleasure, as we have seen, is an instance, that can move to action.

From this last point it would seem to follow that in any account of action—in other words, in an account of even the most complex type of action—the self, or universal side to volition, will in part at least be represented by pleasure. And this is indeed Bradley's position. What is distinctive about the account of appetite is that the pleasure to which it makes reference is of so peculiarly primitive a kind. But that only records—

[1] Ibid., pp. 263–8.

though it does not exhaust—the fact that the type of self that appetite presupposes is itself a primitive type of self: a fact that Bradley brings out when he says, as he does repeatedly, that in appetite the self 'affirms' itself—affirms, that is, not 'realizes', itself.

Now, I would contend that it is prima facie a strength of Bradley's account of action and its volitional structure that, even on its lowest level, it accommodates some form of self: just as I would also add, parenthetically this time, that it is prima facie an advantage for any developmental psychology, like, say, psychoanalytic theory, if it can postulate, from even the ̬earliest stages of mental life, an ego however rudimentary.[1] But I say prima facie in both cases: for this lead can be maintained only if a further, genetic thesis is provided, itself involving only perspicuous transitions, showing how what is presumed present from the beginning evolves into its final, complex form. And it would be my claim that out of what Bradley has to say in the original text of *Ethical Studies* and in the additional material appended nearly fifty years later in 1924, can be reconstructed just such a genetic thesis, taking one from the primitive self that affirms itself in appetite to the good self that realizes itself in moral action.

Ostensibly what Bradley does is to provide a systematic account of different types of action, in which each type is more complex than its predecessor, and where difference in type of action is paired off with difference in type of object of volition. He produces what may be thought of as a hierarchy either of action or of object of volition. However, in doing this Bradley also provides, I claim, a genetic thesis about the self, because at each new level in the hierarchy, it becomes apparent that a new and more evolved type of self is required into being if the particular and the universal sides of volition are to engage with one another. And this genetic thesis reveals its adequacy for his moral theory in that the most evolved type of self it posits, or the self at the very top of the hierarchy, can reasonably be thought of as realizing itself in willing the most complex object of volition.

But to understand this account we must first grasp what is meant by a type, or, more significantly, by different types, of object of volition. Clearly this is not the same as different objects

---

[1] This is to be taken as the first substantive reference in this lecture to the work of Melanie Klein, with which it will later engage: and the relevant contrast here is with the work of Anna Freud and, on a more sophisticated level, with that of Margaret Mahler and her co-workers.

of volition—presumably the object is of the same type when now I will a plate of smoked salmon as when in childhood I willed a lump of sugar. A reasonable suggestion, seemingly in line with Bradley's thinking, is that we can talk of not just different objects of volition, but different types of object, when and only when there are different objects, and, furthermore, in having—equally in lacking—one of these objects the agent would stand in a quite different relationship to it from what he would stand in to the other, if he had or lacked that: where the terms 'object of volition', 'have', and 'lack' are all used quite schematically and as mutual correlatives.

So: in the case of appetite to have the object of volition is—at any rate approximately—to gain physical mastery over it or to consume it: to lack it is for it to be beyond one's reach. That exemplifies one relationship to the object of volition. But now consider the following sequence of possible ends that an agent might adopt as the object of his volition: one, the presence or proximity of a loved figure in the environment; two, the state of satisfaction or happiness of such a figure; three, conforming to, or ultimately, four, the adoption of, that figure's will and character. If we consider this sequence, it should be apparent that as an agent progressed through it, acquiring new ends, then at each point in the sequence the relationship in which he stood to the object of his volition—stood to it, that is, either in having it or in lacking it—would radically alter; and in describing the agent's movement through this sequence as a 'progression' I have in mind the further, and I hope no less apparent, fact that the relationship of agent to object, as it altered, would also become increasingly more abstractly identified. The pattern that realizes it must be characterized on an even higher level of generality. And it is this that warranted my saying of Bradley that he produces not merely a list of different types of object of volition or a list of different types of action, but a hierarchy. For, of course, readers of Bradley will have recognized, and others of you may have suspected, that the sequence of ends I enumerated just now—the presence of another, the welfare of another, obedience to another, the will of another—was not selected by me at random but corresponds to what Bradley thinks is willed by the agent as he engages in increasingly complex types of action. They are the objects of volition that the appetitive child progressively makes his own.

This being so, we can already see one line of determination along which more complex types of action might be thought to require into being more evolved types of self. For each new type of action requires a self that can form—and, we might add, maintain—a more and more abstract view of what counts as the success, alternatively as the failure, of his will. On the universal side of volition there must be, we might think, some representation of mounting complexity that attaches to the realization of the particular side.

But, if this were so, it would, of course, all lie in the cognitive domain, and it would contribute only to a genetic thesis about a self that emerges or develops intellectually. And the cognitive plays no part, or next to none, in Bradley's moral psychology at least at this stage. The development of the self in which Bradley is specifically interested falls within the emotional domain, and it derives from the way in which, according to him, different types of object of volition, and therefore different types of action, make new demands upon the feelings and desires of the child: more precisely, from the way in which they enlarge his capacity to experience pleasure and pain. And in this connection we may note two distinct, though clearly interrelated, lines of determination.

It would be true, and I hope informative, to say of appetite that the child experiences pleasure in having the lump of sugar only when he wants the sugar and then only because he wants the sugar. Let us now look at these two conditions in perhaps artificial separation. So: 'Only *when* he wants the sugar'—that is, the child takes no pleasure in the object as such: it is for him neither permanently nor independently pleasant.[1] 'And then only *because* he wants the sugar'—that is, the pleasure that the child experiences when he does is always in contrast to some pain that he simultaneously or, more likely, antecedently, experiences. The pleasure—and it is a favoured phrase of Bradley's— the pleasure is 'felt against'[2] the felt absence of the object of appetite. It is then in both these respects that, as the child comes to engage in new types of action, his capacity to experience pleasure (and pain) in relation to the object of volition develops: and this development is in turn crucial for—indeed one might say partly constitutive of—the emergence of the self.

First, then, the child extends the range of objects in which he may take pleasure. And, if I have already indicated how this goes, I should now fill in the detail. It goes, then, from the

---

[1] Bradley remarks wrily, 'It is not pleasant to live in the public room of an inn where eating goes on all day.' Op. cit., p. 268.

[2] Ibid., pp. 266, 267, 283 n.

transient thing that will satisfy appetite, to the same thing conceived of as an enduring object, to a loved person who is always with the child, to the well-being or happiness of such a person, to that person's will or set of precepts, and finally to persons and causes with which the child is not personally involved. At each stage—Bradley is at pains to point out—the extension of what is found pleasant is based firmly on the previous stage. So consider the all-important extension from an object that habitually satisfies appetite to the satisfaction or happiness of a person in the environment. What ensures this transition, according to Bradley, is that there are persons in the environment who are already linked with the habitual satisfaction of the child's appetites. It is, he says, 'a fact which deserves more attention than it receives'[1] that the first figures to whom the child is permanently attached are those who have satisfied his first recurring wants and are a fixed aspect of the environment. And he specifies mother and nurse.

Bradley is anxious that the growth of 'interest'—as he calls it, following Hegel—should be safe against two fairly ready misinterpretations. It is not the case, he insists, that this process depends—as some eighteenth-century moralists would have us think—on the workings of sympathy: so that the child's pleasure is caused by another's pleasure through the intervention of associated ideas, first of the other's pleasure, then of the child's. For apart from the question whether such a mechanism could indeed account for the result required of it, appeal to it denies the basic fact that the child's pleasure in new objects is as direct as any it received from satisfied appetite. But nor is it the case, Bradley also insists, that the child simply remains confined to the pleasure of satisfied appetite, and that its interest in other people, their happiness, their injunctions, their aims, is no more than a cultivation of these various things as means to a pleasure distinct from them.

Bradley's own account of the extension of interest is in terms of objectified feeling. So an object excites pleasure in a child, and he then comes to invest this object with that feeling, so that from then onwards he experiences the object in much the same way as up till then he had experienced his sensations of satisfied appetite. He feels it 'as part of himself':[2] or again, without it he 'does not "feel his self"' at all'.[3] And the point is illustrated,

[1] Ibid., p. 284.
[2] Ibid., p. 284.
[3] Ibid., p. 282.

in a way that may remind us of later theory, thus: 'The breast of his mother, and the soft warmth and touches and tones of his nurse, are made one with the feeling of his own pleasure and pain.'[1] If, Bradley maintains, an explanation of this process is still demanded in terms of ideas and their vicissitudes, then we should think not that the ideas of the object and my pleasant feelings are associated, but that the two ideas are integrated or become one: though Bradley might have been wise to point out that this is not so much an explanation, as a consequence or register, of the objectification of feeling.

So much for the first way in which, as the child comes to engage in new types of action, his capacity to experience pleasure and pain in relation to the object of volition develops. Interest enlarges, or the range of object in relation to which he experiences direct pleasure extends beyond that which satisfies transient appetite.

Secondly, as this occurs, the pleasure that the child experiences in the object is no longer felt against, or is no longer felt exclusively against, pain. There are three considerations relevant here, for two of which we have already been prepared. The first is that, as we move up the scale of action, the requirement to find a place for pain in the account of volition weakens. When to have the object of volition means, as in appetite, to possess it physically, then the equation of lacking the object with being deprived of it or the sense of privation, which is painful, is plausible. But as having the object is increasingly a matter first of doing something or other, and then of being something or other, the equation loses plausibility. And at the same time—and this is the second consideration—the child is increasingly drawn to the object for its own sake, so that he takes pleasure in it because of what it is, and permanently is, rather than, as in appetite, because of how he is and transiently is. But the third consideration is the most important. And that is that, as the scope of interest enlarges, as feeling comes to be widely objectified, as the significance of the object becomes increasingly independent of the child's immediate state, so the relevant background to any single action of his lengthens, so that it now takes in not just the fact that here and now he lacks the object of volition but also the fact that on repeated occasions in the past he has had the object. Past satisfactions are now stored: for it is no longer the case that satisfaction endures only until want returns, but it is somehow laid down in external achievement or internally in

[1] Ibid., p. 172.

the form of character and habits, and thus realized is perpetually pleasant. 'The child', Bradley says, 'has done something; and what he has done he still in some shape or other has, if it be only in credit; he possesses an objective issue of his will, and in that not only did realize himself, but does perpetually have himself realized.'[1]

IV

This last quotation might suggest that, in Bradley's eyes, we have now reached a self of the relevant complexity that, insert it on to the universal side of a volitional structure, see that an appropriate end occupies the particular side, and we can think of the ensuing action as self-realization. However, it is his view that, before this can be seen to be correct, we must add to the account of the self—to the account of the self, I say, rather than to the self, for it may be that a self that will satisfy the account thus far given, will satisfy the rest—two further stipulations. The first is that there should be knowledge of good and evil and the corresponding capacity to will each as such. And the second is the division of the self into the good self and the bad self. The two conditions, or the processes that lead up to them, for each is the product of slow growth, are intimately connected.

'The existence of two selves in a man', Bradley writes, 'is a fact which is too plain to be denied.'[2] Two selves, note, aiming respectively at the good and the bad, and not just two collections of desires, some of which we happen to think good and the others bad. In the beginning, however, these two selves are represented in the young child by something like two centres of pleasure, of which one is under the influence of the extension of interest, while the other is not. Given the role of pleasure in volition—and we have seen something of this—the consequences of there being two such centres within the child should be discernible. Not only will he act upon different desires at different times, not only will action upon these different desires establish within him different habits, but at these different times the world will seem to him so different that it will not occur to him to will otherwise than as he does. And at times the two centres can be so brought into conjunction that the world will seem to him these two different ways at one and the same time.

A crucial stage, however, in the development of the two selves out of the two centres of pleasure is reached when interest has

[1] Ibid., p. 289.
[2] Ibid., p. 276.

grown to the point when the precepts and prohibitions—the will, in other words—of a loved figure become the object of the child's volition. This stage is crucial for two reasons.

In the first place, the conflict between the two sets of desires, issuing from the two centres, always active, now becomes sharpened: and that is because one set is now experienced as conforming to, whereas the other set is recognized as contravening, this will. And the conflict is then further sharpened as the will, originally, of course, encountered as external, or as 'the will of the superior', in Bradley's words 'ceases to be external and becomes autonomy'.[1] And, secondly, it is at this stage, and not coincidentally, that the child acquires knowledge of good and evil, and, once the knowledge has been acquired, good and evil are then appropriated by the centres, so that each centre has now a distinctive and unified way of expressing its aim. So, to put the two reasons together, not only is the conflict between the two sets of desire accentuated, it now gains a new self-consciousness.

I said that it was not coincidental that it was at this stage, as internal conflict grows, that Bradley thought that the child acquired knowledge of good and evil. What I had in mind was Bradley's insistence that good and bad can never be known, nor ideas of them acquired, from something purely external. The modern absurdity of 'moral education', which occupies some contemporary philosophers of morals and of education, finds no place in his thinking. 'Knowledge of morality', Bradley insists,

is knowledge of specific forms of the will, and, just as will can be known only because we know our will, so these forms of will demand personal and immediate knowledge. Hatred of evil means feeling of evil, and you can not be brought to feel what is not inside you, or has nothing analogous within you. Moral perception must rest on moral experience.[2]

The relevance of this important idea in the present context is this: that, if, initially, the division of the self into a good self and a bad self is facilitated by the child's learning of good and evil, under which ideas the two selves can then organize themselves, nevertheless, once this knowledge has been acquired, facilitation will occur in the other direction. The child's knowledge of good and evil will be further deepened by the felt division of the self into good and bad, and by the recurrent experience of internal conflict:

[1] Ibid., p. 301.
[2] Ibid., p. 298.

It will not do for the subject merely to be identified with good on the one side, bad on the other, to perceive their incompatibility and feel their discrepancy. He cannot know them unless he knows them against each other.[1]

V

There are two distinct parts of Melanie Klein's theory that contribute to our understanding of morality, and these also, I wish to suggest, by conforming to Bradley's moral psychology go some way to underpinning it: these are the account of internal objects, and the account of the depressive position. In arguing for their relevance to Bradleian theory I shall consider the two accounts in turn.

In discussing Bradley's ideas I made no attempt to relate British Idealism to the philosophy of Hegel. Similarly in discussing Mrs. Klein's ideas I shall not attempt the hotly debated question precisely how the English school of Psychoanalysis relates to Freud's own theory—though it is my own conviction, which I shall therefore state baldly, that one is the proper continuation of the other. But, however the question is to be decided in general, it is clear that the Kleinian account of internal objects takes off from certain hypotheses of Freud's about the development of the ego, initially put forward in two of his greatest papers, 'On Narcissism' and 'Mourning and Melancholia',[2] and then more systematically presented in *Group Psychology and the Ego*.[3] So: in order to explain internal objects and their formation Mrs. Klein invoked just what Freud had invoked to explain the watching, measuring, criticizing agency that occupied him in the Narcissism paper and also the lost love-object incorporated in the ego which he thought to be at the base of melancholia. In both cases appeal is made, on the one hand, to the appropriate developmental state of the instincts, including anxiety, and, on the other hand, to a few psychic mechanisms, of which clearly the most relevant is introjection. And, as these examples suggest, the strength of the explanation must lie, in part, in the wide range of phenomena it can account for, from the case where a bad object is taken in defensively, so as to ward off anxiety, to that where a good object is taken in constructively, so as to strengthen or extend mental structure.

[1] Ibid.
[2] Sigmund Freud, *Complete Psychological Works*, ed. James Strachey, etc. (London, 1953–74), vol. xiv.
[3] Ibid., vol. xviii.

One significant respect in which Mrs. Klein goes beyond what Freud explicitly asserts, though not beyond what he suggests, is in what she has to say about how the various psychic mechanisms operate, or in what mental activity their functioning consists, and her view is that in each case their functioning consists in phantasy.[1] More precisely it consists in phantasy twice over. For—suppose we concentrate on introjection—then the initial incorporative process can be identified with a phantasy of ingesting the object through the contemporaneously dominant bodily zone or channel: say the mouth, or possibly the anus. And, then as a consequence of this initial phantasy there is set up in the mind of the person who has entertained it a disposition to entertain further phantasies in which a counterpart object to the object internalized—an internal object—is represented as being —that is, as living or dying—inside one.

If it is now asked how this mental activity, phantasy, is to be understood, the suggestion most in keeping with Kleinian theory is that it should be understood as a piece, occurrent or dispositional, of imaginative activity, normally unconscious, and engaged in (and this we shall see is important) under a belief in the omnipotence of thoughts. Elsewhere I have argued for this interpretation,[2] but this evening I wish only to indicate a particular advantage that it has for us. And that is that it can account for a distinction, of general importance for psychoanalytic theory, but peculiarly relevant for our concerns, between two types of introjection.[3] One, which is identification, concludes with the internal object represented as within, or part of, the self: the other, which might be called mere internalization, concludes with the internal object represented as over and against the self; and my suggestion about the nature of phantasy would then explain this distinction by reference to a difference, phenomenologically accessible, between two kinds of imaginative activity—that is, between the case where one imagines someone else 'from the inside', or one imagines him centrally, and the case where one imagines oneself centrally and someone else from the outside, or one imagines him peripherally. For, within the dispositional piece of phantasy, which is relevant here, one could then pair off

[1] e.g. *The Writings of Melanie Klein*, ed. Roger Money-Kyrle, etc. (London, 1975–   ), vol. i, p. 291.

[2] Richard Wollheim, 'Identification and Imagination', in *Freud: A Collection of Critical Essays*, ed. Richard Wollheim (New York, 1974).

[3] Perhaps the most thorough and systematic discussion of these distinctions is to be found in Roy Schafer, *Aspects of Internalization* (New York, 1968).

identification with imagining someone else centrally, and mere internalization with imagining someone else peripherally.[1]

But let me explain what I meant by saying that the distinction within introjection is peculiarly relevant for our concerns. I meant that the Bradleian account of the development of the moral self out of a more primitive self seems to presuppose something very like identification, and once we have the structure of this mechanism reasonably straight, then we can, by appending it to that account, make that account at once clearer and stronger.

The first and most obvious place where identification fits on to the Bradleian account is in connection with the growth of 'interest'. (And it is noteworthy, though no more than that, that Bradley himself makes much use of the term 'identification' in connection with the extension of interest.) For recall that Bradley rules out two possible interpretations of this process: one is that the child engages in some complex piece of ratiocination in which he puts himself in another's place so that then pleasure will accrue to him, the other that he remains incorrigibly selfish and attends to another's pleasure but only to ensure, consequentially, his own. And perhaps we can see how identification, interpreted as I have suggested, is well calculated both to bring about the requisite result and to do so without mediation. For it will ordinarily be the case—that is, outside phantasy— that the child, by centrally imagining someone else, will, if he feels anything, feel what the person whom he imagines would, or would be believed to, feel. If the child felt otherwise, this would destroy the centrality of that person in his imagination. And what phantasy adds to this ordinary linkage, is that, by requiring that the imaginative activity is engaged in under the belief in the omnipotence of thoughts, it ensures that the child feels something. He will feel something, that is, unless he is too psychically damaged to feel at all: and then we would think of him as also too damaged to phantasize. And if he does feel what the person whom he centrally imagines would feel, his emotional range will enlarge.

My suggestion then is that one part of Kleinian theory—the theory of internal objects—allows us a better insight into a phenomenon vital to the development of the self—the extension of interest—which Bradleian moral psychology merely asserts.[2]

[1] Richard Wollheim, op. cit.
[2] This is not, of course, literally true. But in this lecture I have deliberately left out of account whatever advantage Bradley's moral theory seeks to derive from the metaphysical view that humanity is a concrete universal or that

But probably other psychological theories or fragments of such theories could do this, and therefore how strong a claim to relevance Kleinian theory can make must depend on the extent to which in explaining one aspect of Bradleian moral psychology it can also explain others.

Now, if within Bradleian moral psychology the emergent self characteristically comes to seek pleasure in new ends, or rather new types of end, it is no less characteristic of it that, as it finds the pleasure that it seeks, it ceases to feel this exclusively or even predominantly 'against' pain. And this, as we have seen, for three reasons: the pain of privation becomes less in evidence; the pleasure in the object gains in intrinsicality; and past pleasures are now somehow stored in the self and perpetually available to it. And my next suggestion is that this aspect too of the development of the self finds an explanation in the Kleinian account of internal objects, though the explanation it offers requires us to adjust somewhat our over-all view of the matter.

For, let us first note that the new relations between pain and pleasure that Bradley writes of seem to correspond very closely to a certain constellation of emotional attitudes and capacities that Mrs. Klein identifies as the diminution of frustration, the increasing capacity for good experiences, and—most significant in her view—the growing security that the child derives from its knowledge of past satisfactions. And this constellation she not only associates with, but also hopes to explain by reference to, the stable establishment within the ego of a good internal object. And, if we wonder why this should be so, why lasting identification should bring in train these benign consequences, the answer in part rests with what it is that on Kleinian theory is introjected. For the object in the external world that is taken in in phantasy is not simply that which transiently gratifies the infant's appetite, it is, rather, the permanent source of that which gratifies appetite. In the most archaic (and therefore the most significant) case, it is not milk that the infant introjects: it is the breast.

But, if it is true that the account of internal objects can be used to explain both the growth in interest and the new relations between pleasure and pain, what is also true—and this is what I meant by an adjustment to our over-all view of the matter—is that in explaining both phenomena the account establishes what had so far been lacking: this is, a priority between them. For the new relations between pleasure and pain now take precedence,

the individual self is properly seen as part of a larger whole from which it is a mere abstraction. I do not regret this omission.

structurally and hence temporally, over the growth in interest. And this is so because, whereas the new relations between pleasure and pain derive from the mere establishment of the internal object, or from the initiating part of the phantasy, the growth of interest derives from the ongoing part of the phantasy, or from the relations with—that is, the relations in phantasy with—the internal objects.

But it is now time for us to take a closer look at the initiating phantasy itself: the phantasy of incorporation. For that phantasy reflects or represents what in my reconstruction of Bradley I called a particular kind of object of volition: and the point I want to make now is that the phantasy of incorporation represents a fairly primitive kind of action in that the whole associated pattern of what it is to have, and what it is not to have, the object of volition is rudimentarily conceived. It is not the most primitive kind of action, such that having the related object is equated with consuming it, for some objectification of feeling would appear to have occurred. (What is introjected is not milk, but the breast.) Nevertheless it falls within the stage of appetite, and this allows me to make my next point: and that is that the Kleinian account of internal objects provides us with a smooth uninterrupted sequence of events, which starts in a primitive type of action, goes through the incorporative phantasy model-led on this type of action, through the constellation of feelings that this phantasy sets up, through the ongoing phantasy in which the introjected object makes its appearance, through the growth of interest that this ongoing phantasy then permits, and closes on new and more evolved types of action in which the child transcends appetite. In other words, on just one assumption Kleinian theory strings together into a single perspicuous story events that Bradleian moral psychology also insists, though without indicating how, must be connected by only easy or natural transitions. And the one assumption that Kleinian theory makes, which is, of course, totally unrealistic in the short run, but reasonable on a longer term, is that regression does not occur, and it is certainly worth any curious reader's while to ob-serve how close in spirit are what the two theories have to say about how such disturbance or inhibition may occur. What Bradley refers to as Lust—an 'unfortunate' term, he later admitted,[1] meaning, I suppose, totally misleading—and what Mrs. Klein refers to as Envy, are both essentially rooted in insatiability, and their phenomenology is described in surprisingly similar terms.

[1] Bradley, op. cit., p. 269 n.

And now in relating Kleinian theory to Bradleian moral psychology, I have allowed the account of internal objects to overrun that of the depressive position, to which I now turn.[1] In broad outline the depressive position arises when the infant comes to perceive that the good and bad objects with which it has felt itself to be surrounded are really only part-objects or aspects of one and the same thing which therefore has at different times been loved or hated. In venting its rage upon the hated mother the child has in reality or (worse) in omnipotent phantasy damaged the mother it loves. Two broad possibilities are open to it. On the one hand, the infant may be unable to tolerate the perception, and then resorts to such crude mechanisms as splitting or denial, or alternatively to the manic defence. On the other hand, it may be able to accept the perception, and then under the influence of guilt or depressive (as opposed to persecutory) anxiety it will struggle to repair, preserve, or revive the loved injured object. And 'loved injured object' here covers both external and internal objects: for as the child's perception of the external world is corrected to take in whole objects, the inner world is correspondingly modified in its representation. Now, in claiming that the growth of interest, and in consequence the capacity to engage in new types of action, can be explained in terms of the infant's relations with its internal objects, I must be understood as referring to those relations only in so far as they are motivated by the emotions and anxieties characteristic of the depressive position. And in order to grasp the full contribution of the depressive position to the growth of the moral life, one must further appreciate that some of the reparative activity in which the infant engages will be of a symbolical character: that is to say, it will express itself in external creativity and achievement, and, internally, in trying to reclaim lost or split-off parts of the self, and to harmonize the desires with which the infant can readily feel simply assailed. The ego, no longer preoccupied with preserving itself, can attempt to integrate itself.

VI

Certainly the most striking feature in common between the moral psychology of Bradley and that of Mrs. Klein is their connection of the good, or the idea of the good, with harmony or

[1] The formulation of the depressive position and the contrast between depressive and persecutory anxiety is first given in 'Psychogenesis of Manic-Depressive States' to be found in *The Writings of Melanie Klein*, vol. i.

unity, and when, now sixteen years ago, I wrote a book on the philosophy of Bradley this was the only point of comparison that I made.[1] In favour of this connection, and of the associated view that the bad is primarily directed against the good, and the bad is deficient in harmony or unity, all of which might conveniently, though perhaps not all that precisely, be summarized as the thesis of the dependence of the bad upon the good, our two thinkers have, of course, very different arguments; very different considerations weigh with them; and instead of enumerating and correlating these arguments—which would require another lecture to itself—I shall just make certain rather general observations about the thesis that they are designed to support.

First, let me make clear, in case it is not so already, that the thesis is not necessarily a bland or optimistic thesis. Mrs. Klein, for instance, combined a belief in the dependence of the bad on the good with the attribution to the child of phantasies quite incompatible with the sweet and repressive myth of early innocence. Writing of the first few months of life, she describes the situation thus:

> In its oral-sadistic phantasies the child attacks its mother's breast, and the means it employs are its teeth and jaws. In its urethral and anal phantasies it seeks to destroy the inside of the mother's body, and uses its urine and faeces for this purpose. In this second group of phantasies the excrements are regarded as burning and corroding substances, wild animals, weapons of all kinds, etc.; and the childs enters a phase in which it directs every instrument of its sadism to the one purpose of destroying its mother's body and what is contained in it.[2]

But that this is compatible with what I have called the thesis of the dependence of the bad upon the good emerges when we consider what the theory tells us are the objects of the child's sadism or that which it is directed upon. Originally turned against the ego, in which form it is properly identified as the death-instinct, when deflected outwards infantile aggression, or envy as it came to be thought of, flows along one or other of two reasonably distinct channels, both of which can be said to be, in the first instance, laid down by the good or the libidinal. So, if, for instance, it is directed against the breast, a typical infantile target, then it is so either because, though the breast once had the power to satisfy the infant's desires, it seemingly no longer can, or because it possesses an unlimited flow of riches but it

---

[1] Richard Wollheim, *F. H. Bradley* (London, 1959).
[2] *The Writings of Melanie Klein*, vol. i, p. 253.

keeps this for its own, or another's (say, the father's) gratification. 'Envy spoils the primal good object' is the relevant formula.[1]

But, mere misunderstandings to one side, I want to say something very general about the place of the thesis of the dependence of the bad upon the good in our moral thinking, and, in doing so, I shall concentrate for the moment on its most significant constituent—the ultimate unity of the good—and then say this: that, whatever initial implausibility it may possess, some such belief as this, taken very roughly and therefore in need of much refinement, is a prerequisite of a certain form of naturalism to which both our thinkers subscribe and which, I am inclined to think, is not only the one form in which naturalism is acceptable but the form in which it is correct. Indeed, I would think that one might profitably use the tenability or otherwise of this form of naturalism as a sort of test for the thesis.

The form of naturalism to which I refer has nothing to do with the analysis of the moral judgement, which in this century is the locus where naturalism has characteristically set itself up. The naturalism I have in mind concerns the origins of morals, and its claim is that, in so far as the distinction that we ordinarily draw between what is good and what is bad is licit—and already we can see that this kind of naturalism leads to a critical or revisionary ethical theory—this distinction derives from the way in which our earliest feelings, desires, and wishes represent themselves to us. For they represent themselves to us from the beginning as—and here, of course, our vocabulary will be necessarily inadequate—either favourable, comforting, benign, or as unfavourable, harsh, divisive. Take our desires, for instance: these do not present themselves to us, their owners, as simply being what they are for, and all—innocently, one might say— begging for satisfaction as vociferously as their strength determines. On the contrary, some are acceptable, familiar to us, whereas others stand apart from us, for all their force and fury. Now it seems to me a requirement of the view that morality presupposes some more primitive way in which our endowed propensities are experienced favourably or unfavourably, that those of our propensities that we do experience in a favourable light should be on the whole those which are, and are held to be, reconcilable. In this connection, however, it is surely a genuine gain in realism that in the elaboration of such a naturalism

---

[1] Ibid., vol. iii, p. 186.

Kleinian theory adds to the materials with which Bradley's moral psychology makes do the experience of depressive anxiety or guilt and the desire to restore, or create anew, an internal harmony.

It is, moreover, only in the context of this naturalism that I can explain an omission in this lecture, which is deliberate. For I have ignored a topic on which Bradley has little to say but Mrs. Klein has a very great deal to say. And the topic is heteronomy, or the mental phenomenon whereby precepts are given to the agent internally but as if from another, where, in other words, the commander from whose mouth they issue is phantasized peripherally; and the reason for the omission is that it seems totally in keeping with the thought of Bradley, and the view is quite explicit in Mrs. Klein, that such forms of internal regulation, extremely effective though they may be, do not necessarily contribute to our sense of the distinction between good and bad, in so far as this is licit. It is largely due to the misunderstanding of certain remarks of Freud's that it has come to be thought that the conception of the super-ego—a term not so far heard this evening—has a systematic connection with the development of morality. The term 'super-ego' has a not uncomplicated history in Mrs. Klein's theory, as her editors have recently made clear, but it was a constant theme in her thinking that the injunctions or fulminations of internal figures not lying at the core of the ego, play at the best an unreliable, at the worst a deleterious, role in the moral life.

VII

This is all that can be said about the moral psychology of British Idealism and the English School of Psychoanalysis in the time available. I conclude with some observations about the worth of saying it.

My proximate motive in setting what Kleinian theory has to say about the development of the self by the side of the Bradleian account was to make the point that in doing all that he thought he could do for his ethical theory Bradley was appealing to what must be regarded as psychology. The case that he presents for the theory of self-realization rests heavily on substantive issues concerning the mind. But, of course, I would not have thought to subject you to what you have heard this evening unless I had felt that the Bradleio-Kleinian form of inquiry is somehow on the right lines, nor would I have been quite unapologetic in imposing it on you under the heading of a lecture in the history of philosophy, had I not also felt that the example of moral philosophy pursued as a branch of psychology is one to be taken very seriously indeed. But why do I feel this?

Suppose we start, as (and I use both senses of the phrase) the better part of twentieth-century moral philosophy has done, from the other end of the line: with the view that moral philosophy has nothing to do with substantive issues and is essentially involved with the analysis of the moral judgement. Sooner or later such a view encounters this difficulty: that it is possible to devise a judgement that satisfies the analysis, and yet is clearly unacceptable as a moral judgement because, say, its content is too trivial, alternatively the only reasons that anyone could have for holding it true would be arbitrary, perverse, inhuman, or some such. And so the original view of moral philosophy might give way to another, broader view on which its subject-matter is not just the analysis, but, more comprehensively, the nature, of the moral judgement: where the nature of a judgement comprehends the general implicatures of the judgement, and also, perhaps, the characteristic speech-acts directed upon it. But difficulties are not at an end: for however deep an understanding moral philosophy might gain of the nature of the moral judgement, the question of its peculiar authority, of what it can stir up in us, cannot be fully answered within the limits that the present view of the subject imposes. Even if we know everything about what constrains the moral judgement, we shall still not know what about it constrains us. Another way of putting the point would be that the so-called autonomy of the moral judgement, which an 'internalist' account of morality is supposed to grasp, can be grasped only if the account assumes an agent to whom it has first attributed, under the guise of rationality, all the requisite moral attitudes, sentiments, and anxieties.

Now this last consideration suggests a fairly considerable shift in our view of moral philosophy, and in the direction of psychology: so that on the revised view its task is, amongst other things no doubt, to exhibit those beliefs, desires, and related attitudes, which would indeed make moral action—from the agent's point of view, that is—rational. But this view too runs into several difficulties. In the first place, a great deal about morality will remain unsaid if we fix our attention entirely on what moves the agent to moral action: we surely need to attend to what he experiences if he desists from moral action, and also to what there is to morality that also moves him to resist moral action. Secondly, if we concentrate on what moves the agent to moral action, a great deal about morality will have been presupposed: for many of the beliefs, desires, and other attitudes invoked to rationalize moral action will be themselves, in some broad or even narrow sense, the products of morality. Thirdly, and more obscurely, the rationalization of moral action must involve reference—as, indeed, must the rationalization of all action to some degree or other—not only to the beliefs, desires, and attitudes of the agent, but also to how he stands to them, and in particular to how he stands to the desires: to whether (to recycle that phrase) he does or does not identify with them.

And this third difficulty specifically suggests yet another view of moral philosophy, which would permit it not only to take account of the first two difficulties but also to evade a further objection that might have occurred to you: the objection that this last view robs moral philosophy of the universality and conceptual character that we look for in philosophical inquiry. And the new view would be that the central task of moral philosophy—for, again, there will be other tasks—is to explore the nature or structure of that process whereby our propensities, supremely our desires, are modified or selected, our attitudes to them are developed, so that we are then capable of being appropriately moved to moral action.

Such a view of moral philosophy is, of course, precisely designed to meet the third objection against the last view: the objection, that is, that the view does not take account of how we stand to what rationalizes our actions, and specifically of how we stand to our desires. But in meeting this objection the new view also goes some way towards meeting the first two objections. Unlike its predecessor it can take full account of the ambiguities and ramifications of moral action, and it does not have to presuppose morality in the account it gives. It can do all this just because it brings into the centre of attention not a synchronic slice of the agent's mind but a diachronic process in which his mind evolves. Thus it retains moral philosophy within psychology, but relocates it. However, if it retains moral philosophy within psychology, it also reinstates it as a conceptual inquiry. For one way of viewing the psychological process under exploration is as that process which provides the appropriate conditions for the application of the concept or concepts of morality, and indeed moral philosophy is concerned with the process only in so far as it does lead to this outcome. In this respect it seems to me that moral philosophy is in a very similar position to that occupied by the philosophy of the self, whose topic of inquiry is also a process. It may indeed be that it is with one and the same process that the two branches of philosophy are concerned, the difference being that the process is viewed in the two cases with different interests in mind. Such a conclusion is fairly close to the approach of our two thinkers this evening. But, however that may be, in the case both of moral philosophy and of the philosophy of the self, the depth to which philosophical inquiry must cut into the process itself, or how far it should engage with substantive issues, will depend on the estimate one makes of how implicated the sense of the relevant concepts is in the empirical theory under which the process falls.

I end on a question: Is it ironical, or is it by some happier coincidence, that, if one takes the most austerely anti-psychological ethical theory of our day, the imperativist theory, the point at which it seems to come closest to our moral intuitions—that is, where it makes reference to the self-addressed command—is precisely where it conforms to an important truth of moral psychology and one which has been considerably exposed this evening: that morality begins only where the interior dialogue breaks out, a dialogue which on the Bradleian account engages just the good self and the bad self, and which in Kleinian theory pulls in the more numerous and ethically more ambiguous figures of the inner world?

INDEX